JASON STATHAM

JASON STATHAM
TAKING STOCK

LEN BROWN

Copyright © Orion 2011

This edition first published in Great Britain in 2011 by
Orion Books
an imprint of the Orion Publishing Group Ltd
Orion House, 5 Upper St Martin's Lane,
London WC2H 9EA
An Hachette UK Company

10 9 8 7 6 5 4 3 2 1

A CIP catalogue record for this book is available
from the British Library.

ISBN: 978 1 409 1 32653

Typeset by Input Data Services Ltd, Bridgwater, Somerset

Printed and bound in the UK by CPI Mackays, Chatham, Kent

The Orion Publishing Group's policy is to use papers that
are natural, renewable and recyclable and made from wood
grown in sustainable forests. The logging and manufacturing
processes are expected to conform to the environmental
regulations of the country of origin.

Every effort has been made to fulfil requirements with
regard to reproducing copyright material. The author and
publisher will be glad to rectify any omissions at the earliest
opportunity.

www.orionbooks.co.uk

CONTENTS

LIST OF ILLUSTRATIONS

Jason Statham and Stephen Graham in *Snatch*. (COLUMBIA / SKA FILMS / THE KOBAL COLLECTION / PEARSON, SEBASTIAN)

Jason Statham as Frank Martin in *The Transporter*. (20TH CENTURY FOX / THE KOBAL COLLECTION / ENGLISH, JACK)

Mark Wahlberg and Jason Statham talk on the set of *The Italian Job* on 5 October 2002 in Hollywood, California. (Photo by Ben-Ari Finegold/Getty Images)

Seth Green and Jason Statham during the world premiere of *The Italian Job* at Grauman's Chinese Theatre in Hollywood, California, United States. (Photo by SGranitz/WireImage)

Kelly Brook and Jason Statham during MTV Movie Awards 2004 at Sony Pictures Studios in Culver City, California, United States. (Photo by SGranitz/WireImage)

Jason Statham as Frank Martin in *Transporter 2*. (EUROPACORP / TF1 CORP / THE KOBAL COLLECTION)

Jason Statham and Guy Ritchie on the set of *Revolver*. (EUROPACORP / THE KOBAL COLLECTION)

Jason Statham plays Chev Chelios in *Crank*. (LIONS GATE FILMS / THE KOBAL COLLECTION)

Jason Statham and Saffron Burrows in *The Bank Job*. (ARCLIGHT FILMS / RELATIVITY MEDIA / THE KOBAL COLLECTION)

Jason Statham attends the UK premiere of *The Bank Job* at the Odeon West End on 18 February 2008 in London, England. (Photo by Fred Duval/FilmMagic)

Ray Winstone, Mickey Rourke and Jason Statham attend the Cinema Society and Entertainment Weekly screening of *The Wrestler* after party at the Soho Grand Hotel on December 8, 2008 in New York City. (Photo by Dimitrios Kambouris/WireImage)

Jason Statham poses for a portrait shoot while attending Cannes Film Festival on 18 May 2007 in Cannes, France. (Photo by MJ Kim/Getty Images)

Costas Mandylor, Vinnie Jones and Jason Statham attend the Soccer For Survivors Celebrity Soccer Match held at Beverly Hills High School on 22 July 2007 in Beverly Hills, California. (Photo by Barry King/WireImage)

Jason Statham in *Death Race*. (CRUISE / WAGNER PRODUCTIONS / THE KOBAL COLLECTION)

Jason Statham in *Transporter 3*. (TF1 FILMS PRODUCTIONS / THE KOBAL COLLECTION)

Jason Statham in *Crank: High Voltage*. (LIONSGATE / THE KOBAL COLLECTION)

Jason Statham, Randy Couture, Charisma Carpenter, California Gov. Arnold Schwarzenegger, Sylvester Stallone, Terry Crews, Giselle Itie, Dolph Lundgren, Eric Roberts and Steve Austin appear at a screening of *The Expendables* at the Planet Hollywood Resort and Casino 11 August 2010 in Las Vegas, Nevada. (Photo by Ethan Miller/Getty Images)

Sylvester Stallone and Jason Statham in *The Expendables*. (MILENNIUM FILMS / THE KOBAL COLLECTION)

Jason Statham arrives at Planet Hollywood Casino Resort on August 11, 2010 in Las Vegas, Nevada. (Photo by Denise Truscello/WireImage)

Jason Statham in *The Expendables*. (MILENNIUM FILMS / THE KOBAL COLLECTION)

Rosie Huntington-Whiteley attends the Adidas by Stella McCartney presentation and launch of the Spring/Summer 2008 collection on 21 September 2007 in Westway Sports Hall, London, England. (Photo By Nick Harvey/WireImage

Jason Statham films a scene at the *Safe* movie set in Midtown Manhattan on 22 October 2010 in New York City. (Photo by Ray Tamarra/Getty Images)

Jason Statham poses in the awards room at the GQ Men of the Year Awards at The Royal Opera House, on 7 September 2010 in London, England. (Photo by Jon Furniss/WireImage)

ACKNOWLEDGEMENTS

I'd like to express my sincere gratitude to Orion Books for giving me the opportunity to write about Britain's Hollywood action hero. I'd especially like to thank my editor Jane Sturrock for her sound advice, gentle encouragement, serene calmness and great patience during this process. Thanks too to Stephen Fall for his sensitive copyediting and Nicola Crossley for her work on the pictures.

The following individuals and groups have helped me in a variety of supportive ways throughout the autumn of 2010: my in-laws Brian Janet and Rachel Boseley, Alan Jackson and Christine Costello, Chrissie and Bernard Dale, the Southwell Music Users Group, John and Petra Fuller, Charlotte and Nigel Malik, the Three Wee Crows Theatre Company, and the good people of Taynuilt Argyll.

I'd like to dedicate this book to my talented sister Kathleen and my lovely nieces Isla and Maeve Hannigan. Also to my father Drew, now in his tenth decade; an Arnhem veteran, a great father, and an even better grandfather. Keep on keeping on.

Finally, with all my love and heart-felt thanks to my wonderful wife Bridget and our beautiful daughters Grace and Flora. I sincerely apologise for my wild mood swings, badly-shaved head, taciturn table-talk, designer stubble and cavalier driving whilst under the influence of Statham.

'It's been emotional.'

Len Brown, Newcastle-upon-Tyne
x

INTRODUCTION:

BRITAIN'S STEVE MCQUEEN

Precious few British male actors have climbed so far up the greasy pole of the American film industry as quickly as Jason Statham. In the past, being wooed by major Hollywood studios was the preserve of great thespians such as Laurence Olivier and Alec Guinness or stylish leading men from Cary Grant to Michael Caine.

Arguably, British men dominated the industry in the 1960s, led by the likes of Alan Bates, Richard Burton, Albert Finney and Terence Stamp, but generally home-grown Hollywood talent took over in the 1970s – Jack Nicholson, Al Pacino, Dustin Hoffman, Robert De Niro – *and* the 1980s: Sylvester Stallone, Bruce Willis and so on.

More recently, the British stars of youthful movies such as *Harry Potter* (Daniel Radcliffe) and the *Twilight* vampire saga (Robert Pattinson) have been hugely successful. But, aside from the most famous long-running UK film franchise – with its almost royal lineage of actors, from Sean Connery to Daniel Craig, who have played James Bond – few British men have established themselves as major stars in Los Angeles.

It is significant that in the last eighty years, since the ritual began, only thirteen Britons have claimed cinema's ultimate prize, a 'Best Actor' Academy Award: Charles Laughton, Robert Donat, Ray Milland, Ronald Colman (twice), Laurence Olivier (twice), Alec Guinness, David Niven, Rex Harrison, Paul Scofield, Ben Kingsley, Anthony Hopkins, Jeremy Irons and Daniel Day Lewis (twice). Most of these men were classically trained and the majority spoke in Home Counties-style English.There has been no shortage of famous English Oscar nominees – diversely talented characters speaking in a variety of dialects including Peter Sellers, Michael Caine, Albert Finney, John Hurt, Tom Courtenay, Ian McKellen, Bob Hoskins, Ralph Fiennes, Jude Law and Colin Firth – but none of them managed to grab the golden statue. Perhaps this says something about the attitude of the Academy towards British men? Maybe they are so hooked on the 'proper' English accent as delivered by actors from Laughton and Olivier through to Hugh Grant, that they fail to appreciate the different vowel sounds of Britons born outside the Home Counties? Are they just prejudiced against the lower classes?

But it's also interesting to note that many of the Oscar-nominated English actors born north of Watford or west of Surrey were nevertheless dramatically trained at RADA (London's Royal Academy of Dramatic Art), including the Salford lad Albert Finney, Hull's Tom Courtenay and Chester-field's John Hurt. All three were following in the famous footsteps of classical actors such as Charles Laughton, Trevor Howard and Ralph Fiennes.

Of the precious few who weren't RADA-trained, Michael Caine joined the Westminster Rep Company, Ben Kingsley studied at the University of Salford, Jude Law and Daniel Day Lewis developed their talents with the National Youth Theatre, Jeremy Irons started out at the Bristol Old Vic, and Colin Firth enlisted at the Drama Centre in London.

In fact, of all the male, English contenders for Oscars in recent history, arguably only the Lancastrian Ian McKellen and the cockney Bob Hoskins have successfully made the journey to Hollywood without any formal theatrical training whatsoever. To this extraordinary and exclusive list we can now add the name of Jason Statham. Within little more than a decade, without any dramatic coaching and with a voice like an East End bouncer gargling gravel, Jason has rapidly developed into one of Britain's most successful film stars and arguably, ahead of Daniel Craig, he has become the first truly working-class action-adventure hero these islands have produced.

Some would argue that, in the 21st century, action-adventure heroes have become an old-fashioned, out-dated concept; a throwback to the dark days of the 1980s when on-screen warriors such as John Rambo and Rocky Balboa ruled the earth. Could it be true, as some Hollywood critics have claimed, that Jason Statham is indeed the last action hero? Perhaps, but he would probably disagree with the title and might prefer the phrase 'accidental action hero'.

'Where did America's toughs guy go?' the USA magazine *Variety* asked recently.

'Not so long ago, Hollywood's male stars were men's men.

3

Think John Wayne, Robert Mitchum, Humphrey Bogart and Steve McQueen ...'

You could add in the names of other American action stars from the 1980s and 1990s – Harrison Ford, Mel Gibson and Samuel L. Jackson – but, during the first decade of the 21st century, things changed dramatically in Hollywood.

Before the release of *The Expendables* in the summer of 2010, big-budget all-action movies had become a thing of the past. In economically challenging times, LA studios increasingly focused their finances on animated films, such as *Toy Story* and *Shrek*, light-hearted escapist historical adventures (*Pirates of the Caribbean*) and superhero stories (*Iron Man, Batman, Spiderman*). As a result, computer-generated imagery (CGI) and 3-D had become more appealing and exciting to cinema-goers than realistic action sequences; threatening the extinction of the old-style American tough-guy characters.

As *Variety* also observed, 'These days, studios are hard-pressed to find home-grown traditional male leads to carry their pictures. Their star rosters include countless boy-men who, even after they turn forty, are less than credible macho movie stars.' One old-time Hollywood producer, Robert Relyea, backed up *Variety*'s verdict. Having worked with Steve McQueen on *Bullitt* and *The Magnificent Seven*, Relyea complained that now 'You've got copycats trying to be McQueen but they don't get it. McQueen didn't give a damn who his make-up man was. It's not fashionable for actors to be all-American men now.'

If you scan the current star ratings, you'll see that Relyea's conclusion is supported by the box-office receipts for Hollywood's major male actors over the last few years. None of the five big US star attractions – Leonardo DiCaprio, Brad

Pitt, Johnny Depp, Will Smith and George Clooney – would argue that they were action heroes, and behind them there is a strangely diverse mix of characters including Robert Downey Jnr (*Iron Man*, *Sherlock Holmes*), Robert Pattinson, Daniel Radcliffe and (*Avatar* star) Sam Worthington.

Increasingly, America has looked across the Atlantic for tough-guy characters to fill the vacuum in 'men's men', courting brawny Brits such as Gerard Butler (who starred in the Spartan epic *300*) and the brooding Christian Bale as Batman in *The Dark Knight*.

But aside from Sylvester Stallone – the veteran *Rocky* and *Rambo* creator, who battled his way back to the top of the listings with *The Expendables* – the only top-twenty Hollywood actor who could justifiably and convincingly be branded as a 'credible macho movie star' is surely Jason Statham.

Over the past decade Jason has been on an incredible journey from the hustling streets of South London to the high life in the Hollywood Hills and Malibu beach. The son of a market trader, he became an international diver and later a male model, before breaking into acting by playing a key role in *Lock Stock & Two Smoking Barrels*. This was the first of a series of films on which he worked with the maverick young British director Guy Ritchie (who would later become more famous as the husband of Madonna). Such was the closeness of the relationship between Statham and Ritchie that one journalist even wrote 'You begin to think that Guy Ritchie has based five movies all around this man ... he is the man Guy Ritchie wants to be.'

Jason would strongly disagree with this, but he would certainly credit Guy with giving him the chance of a lifetime, initially setting him on course for Hollywood. 'In Britain they don't make action movies except for the Bond franchise, and that's one of the reasons I'm in the States,' he would say in 2008. 'I stuck around in England for years, but I never got an offer to make any film over there, except with my good mate Guy Ritchie. I don't know why the people who make films in the UK haven't embraced me. I think they like people who have fallen out of RADA and come from a traditional background. But we're happy; we're cooking along.'

The partnership with Ritchie, professionally and personally, played a huge part in Jason's transformation from London lad to Hollywood hero. When he moved to Los Angeles in 2000 – with his then-girlfriend, the model, TV presenter and actress Kelly Brook – Ritchie's and Madonna's connections, and the post-*Snatch* friendships he developed with everyone from Vinnie Jones to Brad Pitt, enabled Jason to break into Hollywood films. His early supporting roles in *Turn It Up* and *Ghosts of Mars* began to convince producers that he had the charisma and screen presence to deliver a leading role.

Through meeting his manager Steve Chasman, and working with Chasman's Ace Media clients Jet Li and Corey Yuen, Jason began to reveal his extraordinary talents as a martial artist and an action man, proving that he was physically and mentally strong enough to take on the most demanding challenges. Together with the innovative French writer/director Luc Besson, they created *The Transporter* (2002), introducing a new generation of cinema-goers to the mysterious and fascinating action hero Frank Martin.

As many critics suggested, the *Transporter* and *Bourne* franchises propelled action movies into the new millennium, even prompting more traditional but successful adventures –

including the James Bond films – to update their style, make lead characters more universal and modern in their appeal, and increase the realistic quality of the stunts.

Significantly, the *San Francisco Chronicle* stated that Jason's debut performance as *The Transporter* was reminiscent of old-style Hollywood action and Western heroes such as Clint Eastwood and John Wayne: 'As mercenary Frank in the original *Transporter*, Statham found his ideal role: a tough loner with a glimmer of humanity, like an old-time gunfighter. Even with his English accent, you could easily see this actor riding with the Magnificent Seven.'

Jason built on the cult success of the first *Transporter* with sequels in 2004 and 2008. He also starred as an adrenaline-fuelled action man with a great sense of humour in two hyperactively mad *Crank* films in 2006 and 2008.

But he has also appeared in a wide variety of other genre films over the past decade, including the sporting prison adventure *Mean Machine*, the psychological thriller *Cellular*, the art-house independent feature *London*, the police-corruption drama *Chaos*, martial arts movies *The One* and *War*, the children's fantasy feature *In the Name of the King* and the gritty British crime story *The Bank Job*. Plus, there have been diverse cameos in *Collateral*, *The Pink Panther* and *13*.

Along the way, Jason seems to have deliberately developed an enigmatic, man-of-mystery image both on and off the screen. Outside of his inner circle of family and friends, no one really knows what drives the actor relentlessly onwards and upwards. The very public break-up of his long-term relationship with Kelly Brook sparked a tabloid feeding-frenzy in 2004, reinforcing his determination to keep his personal world truly private. As a result, he has rarely been interviewed about his life away from the film set, preferring to let the acting and the action speak for themselves.

If you wanted to highlight the key moments when Jason quickly stepped up from inexperienced actor and apprentice star into Hollywood's big league then, for different reasons, you would point to three films: *The Italian Job*, *Death Race* and *The Expendables*.

In the 2003 remake of *The Italian Job*, his role as the fast-driving ladies' man Handsome Rob brought him to the attention of a huge American and international audience; the film grossed over $175million at the box office. Although Universal Pictures' 2008 movie *Death Race* wasn't as commercially triumphant, it nevertheless proved Jason could front a major studio Hollywood film, deliver a more complex emotional performance and, above all, showcase his unique stunt-driving action-man skills and his extraordinary physique. Significantly, the original – highly controversial – *Death Race 2000* had starred Sylvester Stallone alongside David Carradine.

In 2009, when Stallone was looking for that rarest of creatures, a credible 21st-century macho Hollywood movie star, he naturally called up Jason Statham. As Stallone said of the rest of his cast of revitalised Expendables, 'We're old, we're like head waiters at the Last Supper ... we had a dinosaur as a heli-pad.' In Jason – who had always admired Sly's work as Rocky and Rambo – Stallone found his present-day action hero; someone current and convincing who could bring in a more youthful audience and even attract a few women to this often male-biased cinema genre. For these reasons, Jason received second billing in the press and publicity among an all-star cast of action goliaths.

Over the years, depending on your personal viewpoint, Jason has either been incredibly fortunate or exceptionally shrewd and perceptive in terms of the productions he has become involved with. Clearly his decision-making process has been based on original ideas, strong scripts, visionary directors, clever casting and great creative teams, but the real evidence of his success is obvious from the on-screen company he has been keeping. He worked alongside Stallone, Bruce Willis, Arnold Schwarzenegger and Mickey Rourke in *The Expendables*, Rourke again in *13*, Robert De Niro and Clive Owen in *The Killer Elite*, Brad Pitt and Benicio del Toro in *Snatch*, Tom Cruise in *Collateral*, Jet Li in *The One* and *War*, Kim Basinger in *Cellular*, Mark Wahlberg, Charlize Theron and Donald Sutherland in *The Italian Job*, Ben Foster and Sutherland again in *The Mechanic*, Ian McShane and Joan Allen in *Death Race*, and Chris Evans and Jessica Biel in *London*.

Whereas most actors who have achieved Jason's level of success and fame might expect nominations for major film awards, he has always been incredibly self-deprecating and light-hearted in his attitude towards his career. Perhaps he underestimates his own onscreen talent? More importantly, he has earned great respect from many of the big-league producers and directors he has worked with. For example, the Frenchman Olivier Megaton, who directed *Transporter 3*, commented that, 'In my eyes, Jason's becoming the new Bruce Willis. He has incredible charisma and he's so physical. He's also a very instinctive actor. He doesn't need to talk – his eyes convey all the emotions he needs to get across.'

Roger Donaldson, director of *The Bank Job* (2008),

observed that 'Jason's like a British Steve McQueen. There's a really great brooding sort of quality about him. He does a lot with a little, and he's very charismatic. He's not like anyone else that I know of on screen.'

Herein lie Jason's strength as a film star. Those who originally believed he was just another British supporting actor in a long-line of loveable 'cor blimey' cockney outlaws, have completely misjudged him. The art of cinema, in contrast to television dramas and soap operas, is to *show* rather than tell what's going on; on the big screen it's all about revelation rather than explanation. Although Jason's natural acting style is sometimes, in a lazy but extremely complimentary way, compared to that of Michael Caine or Bob Hoskins, he has proved himself to be a much more physical actor with a host of admirable stuntman disciplines in his armoury.

This is one of the main reasons he has impressed 1980s action heroes such as Stallone and Willis, and also why he has been courted by major-league movie producers such as Harvey Weinstein. As *GQ*'s Dylan Jones astutely observed, Jason Statham is the ideal man to have onboard your movie in economically challenging times: 'He's the Warren Buffett of the big screen; a nervous studio exec's cast-iron talisman for a healthy return on a hefty investment.'

From Rudolph Valentino to James Dean, from Paul Newman and Steve McQueen to Brad Pitt and Johnny Depp, the most famous film actors have always been classic pin-ups boasting perfect hair and Hollywood smiles, chiselled jaws and well-defined cheek bones. In total contrast, Jason is a very different, arguably more modern, kind of everyman movie star.

As Simon Lewis of the *Daily Mail* wrote, 'He's got the hard-knock background, sandpaper voice and steely physique that means box-office receipts in Iowa, Singapore or Tbilisi.' 'Jason Statham is on the cusp of becoming the biggest action star of his generation,' proclaimed the *Sydney Morning Herald* in July 2008. 'Sylvester Stallone thinks so and the thirty-five-year-old from south-east London has been hailed as a latter-day Steve McQueen – tough and rough but still a total charmer.'

GQ magazine agreed: 'Jason Statham's voice marks him immediately not so much as an alpha male, but as an alpha bloke ... it's gravelly but melodic in that working-class Brit way.' In 2008, Jason admitted that his hard day's night growl comes from 'lots of smoking and drinking'.

It's this man-of-the-people, blue-collar quality, combined with his unconventional lived-in appealing features, that has been central to his success and contributed to Jason's seemingly universal appeal. Aside from playing ass-kicking heroes and world-saving action men he has always come across as a down-to-earth, unpretentious character, both on screen and in the flesh. He has never taken himself too seriously, he distances himself from some of the crazy and unrealistic action roles he plays, and he seems to enjoy meeting his audience because it gives them the chance 'to realise that you are just one of them, that you are just a normal bloke'.

Physically, Jay (as he is known to close friends) or 'The Stath' (as he is often branded by admiring men's fitness magazines) looks very different from many of his A-list contemporaries. Most movie stars, such as DiCaprio, Pitt, Depp and Clooney, are blessed with fine heads of hair. The follically-challenged Bruce Willis comparison obviously comes from the fact that both Jason and Bruce share the same 'grass-doesn't-grow-on-a-busy-street' hairdresser and, like the *Die Hard* hero, Jason has always been more than happy to make fun of his own crazy baldhead image.

He has stated that he 'maintains the stubble on his chin to make up for what he lacks on his head', and when the US chat-show host Jay Leno first showed the poster for *The Expendables* on American television, Jason remarked, 'It looks like a hair-loss commercial.' His *Expendables* co-star Dolph Lundgren was asked if it was ironic that the youngest Expendable was the only one who seemed to be losing his hair? 'You mean Jason Statham?' Dolph laughed. 'Well I don't know if he's losing it or it's just cut short. In the old days, warriors used to have long hair. The power was in the hair, now it's the opposite.'

In the few films in which Jason has either grown some hair or had to wear a wig, notably *Revolver* and *London*, he hasn't looked like himself at all. He even admitted, 'Yeah, it's funny to adopt a bit of head hair.' The greasy, lank, long locks and drooping moustache he wore as Jake Green in *Revolver* made him look like a bad bassist in a 1970s prog-rock band, while the sleek-haired debauched currency-trader style of toupee worn as Bateman in *London* seemed to add to the unsympathetic, angry and unappealing nature of the role.

The bald truth is that the shaven head, combined with the heavy-stubbled face, has become a powerful, often fearsome, image in most of Jason's films; it has helped present him as a believable working-class hero, a vulnerable tough guy, a loner who can definitely take care of himself. If it has become something of a calling card in his cinematic roles, it has also influenced his encounters with the tabloids and the paparazzi.

'It's hard because I've got a recognisable bald head,' he has complained. Perhaps, as a result of being so easily identified, he has been heard to shout 'Oi scumbags!' at predatory press photographers.

Amusingly, when Seth Rogen was asked if he felt like an action hero, having been one of the voices for *Kung Fu Panda*, he joked, 'Oh sure ... Jason Statham, I'm tougher than that guy' before nervously reconsidering his statement and quietly admitting, 'He'll kill me, that guy'll actually murder me! I'll have a big shiny bald head smashed into my nose!' Laughing at this, Jason seemed to confirm Rogan's worst fears: 'It's funny ... I know where he lives so I'm gonna go round and do his windows for him!' He didn't mean with a bucket and sponge.

The tough-guy aura may be why Jason is more popular with female audiences than many of his hard-knock peerage. He has certainly developed a huge male and female fan-base. When he was interviewed on the *Lopez Tonight* American TV show, the host George Lopez told him that 'Dudes like you and women *love* you', to which Jason replied, 'They must need glasses.' And, in modest response to suggestions that, even as a male model, he had looked quite scary, Jason laughed and said, 'I've just got a really bad smile ... I go for the scowl instead.'

American journalists – female members of the press, in particular – have always found Jason to be a fascinating but charming subject. One described a meeting with him as like a 'one-man pub crowd on fight night ... lots of volume, some cheering here and there, plenty of jabs in the air and a dazzling array of casual obscenities'. Having observed him in *Death Race*, Chrissy Iley of *The Times* wrote that 'you can't take your eyes off Statham. It's an intense and internal performance that works well with the hyper-speed action. And you can't take your eyes off his body either. His torso is a work of art.'

It is stating the obvious, but Jason's body has always been one of his greatest strengths, not to mention his talents as a driver, a diver and a martial artist. Although in his early Guy Ritchie films, *Lock Stock & Two Smoking Barrels* and *Snatch*, he wasn't required to impose himself physically on any action in the story; by and large, he left that side of the business to Vinnie Jones or Brad Pitt. But from the turn of the millennium onwards, Jason's extremely high level of fitness and his willingness to execute the most dangerous of stunts have taken him to a unique place in the film industry.

While his contemporaries seem content to allow stunt doubles to do their dirty work, Jason has embraced the challenge in the old-fashioned action-man style of some of his heroes such as Clint Eastwood, Steve McQueen and, particularly, Bruce Lee, feeling that he could convey a greater sense of realism by performing the action scenes himself.

With great intensity and determination, for *Death Race* he trained hard with an ex-member of the US Special Forces and literally transformed his body into a fat-free weapon. 'Anyone who's been an athlete at a certain level knows how to sacrifice and be disciplined and train hard and learn new skill,' he told Helen Barlow of the *Sydney Morning Herald*, as if this 'The Stath'-style physique was somehow within every man's reach. 'I can do it very quickly because I have that mentality and focus.' This single-minded commitment to his career was developed in his formative years, watching actors such as Kirk Douglas in *Spartacus* and Robert De Niro in *Raging Bull*.

Jason has often spoken of his opposition to, and disappointment with, films which rely too heavily on CGI, preferring realistic-looking stunts that are shot by the cameras rather than 'keyed in' during the post-production process. This courageous approach has been in evidence in most of his action film roles, particularly the three *Transporter* films, the two *Crank* films, the martial arts movies with Jet Li and, of course, *The Expendables*. 'I'm like a human bowling ball,' he has admitted. 'I'm always nursing an injury or two but you become immune to the feeling.'

Who but Jason Statham would agree to be filmed dangling from a helicopter by a thin wire 3,000 feet over Los Angeles? Or participate in 160mph car chases? Who else would jump a jet-ski from a river onto a road and then leap onto the back of a moving school bus, just to create an authentic-looking sequence? Or get centrally involved in choreographed but dangerous martial arts battles?

'There's a great reward in doing it yourself,' Jason has said. 'There's no substitute. On-screen they're going to see it's me. You can tell from the fear within me ... the eyes get all glazed, there's adrenaline in your veins.'

Despite his growing pay packet and, inevitably, the increasing costs of insuring him, Jason famously remains the most athletic and most active of action men. This sets him apart from the competition and – even though he has got many other strings to his bow – has clearly made him a unique commodity in 21st-century Hollywood. 'People like to have a label on you and it makes them know what you are,' he once observed. 'I wouldn't really call myself an action star in any of those [Guy Ritchie films]. I've done quite a few films that aren't generated by me kicking the crap out of everybody. It's just that people just see the ones that really excite them, and they go, "Ahh, you're the action guy." I think it also has a lot to do with ... there ain't many people that actually can do it. In my experience, I haven't seen many film actors that can justifiably do what I can. It must be my misspent youth.'

CHAPTER ONE:

THE MAKING OF THE MAN

In the *Transporter* films, Frank Martin emerged as a darkly fascinating, enigmatic and mysterious character. If Clint Eastwood's unshaven gun-slinging stranger was the Man With No Name, then Jason Statham's portrayal of this uncommunicative, fast-driving, street-fighting hero would qualify as the Man With No Past.

In the original *Transporter* movie, the heroine Lai (played by Shu Qi) was seen exploring Frank's Riviera home, finding a box of old photographs, perhaps on the brink of making a discovery about Frank Martin's formative years and his unspoken history. Moments later, all the evidence went up in flames. Throughout all three *Transporter* films we would never learn anything more about Frank's wild early years.

If you tried to research Jason Statham's early life – the life he experienced before he became a leading light in Guy Ritchie's films *Lock Stock & Two Smoking Barrels* and *Snatch*, the years before he became an A-list Hollywood leading man – you'd feel exactly like Lai did about Frank Martin; intrigued, fascinated, attracted and yet always frustrated in terms of who or what he really is and where he has come from. It remains a modern-day mystery. How on earth did this English, working-class boy – who, by his own admission, used to sell knock-off perfumes and jewellery on the streets of London, who used to be a high-board competitive diver for the English team – transform himself into one of the most successful global film stars of the early 21st-century?

In films, all dramatic creations have a back-story; a detailed explanation of their past and present, provided by a novelist or screenwriter outlining imagined key events from childhood and beyond. Back-stories are designed to help actors understand where their character has come from, what their motivation is and where the hell they're going. They inform the performance, make sense of the life decisions each character takes and dictate the way they respond to certain circumstances. The classic example would be Ian Fleming's biographical details of James Bond's background; a Commander in the Secret Services (MI6), born to Scottish banker Andrew Bond and his Swiss wife Monique Delacroix, educated at Sunningdale, Eton and Sandhurst, and with a family motto of *Orbis non suffict* (the world is not enough).

If or when someone comes to play the extraordinary, uneven role of Jason Statham in a biopic, they'll find the mainly-untold back-story confusing and contradictory; like looking at a larger-than-life personality through the wrong end of a telescope; as if the protective layers create greater distance rather than welcome closer attention. Clearly, pursued by modern bounty hunters – those chasing packs of celebrity-raking tabloid journalists – he has carefully covered his tracks, brushing over his footsteps in interviews, rarely talking in detail about who he really is and where he has come from. Out of necessity, like Frank Martin, Jason has chosen to be a man of few words.

Perhaps this has been his wisest career move of all. The history of Hollywood is made up of actors and actresses who have revealed too much of themselves on and off the screen, carelessly displaying their personal weaknesses and limitations to the cinema-going world. They can be viewed as one-dimensional and their careers can become typecast – in, for example, the way Hugh Grant or Jennifer Aniston so often play parts in romantic comedies, or Steven Seagal and Jean-Claude Van Damme have repeatedly appeared in action movies – or, worse still, they can end up playing themselves in ever-less-challenging, predictable or unsatisfying roles.

In many ways it has always proved more fascinating to keep the book closed, like the reclusive Greta Garbo. Mystery enhances star-status and prevents critics and therapists from reading too much into any performance. Given the enigmatic, mostly unknown character that Jason Statham is, it should come as no surprise that even the beginnings of his life are open to some conjecture and confusion. Most sources suggest that he was born on 12 September 1972 in Sydenham, in the London Borough of Lewisham. But, as he never says much about his childhood in interviews, piecing together the early years of Jason's life is somewhat like wandering, lost, in a maze.

A *Chicago Tribune* profile, for example, contained the sentence 'Statham was born in Sydenham, England, and moved around the country from an early age with his parents'. But conflicting information from other sources, one of which is the British Film Institute website, suggests that Jason was born on the same date, but in the mining community of Shirebrook in Derbyshire. A small market town in the Bolsover District of north-east Derbyshire on the border with Nottinghamshire, Shirebrook proudly celebrates Jason as one of the town's most famous sons, alongside the 1966 England World Cup-winning full-back Ray Wilson and the actor John Hurt (whose father was once vicar of the Holy Trinity Parish Church). Close to Mansfield and Chesterfield, the town's fortunes rose and fell with the colliery, which opened in 1896 and closed in 1993.

Wherever Jason was born, it seems to be the case that his childhood years were split between Shirebrook, south-east London and Great Yarmouth. Described in some profiles as being 'Derbyshire at heart', but claimed as a loyal Nottingham Forest fan – probably because of the unfashionable club's great European Cup successes under Brian Clough during his childhood – Jason would spend most of his secondary-school years at Great Yarmouth Grammar School. There, he would begin to excel on the sports field, and particularly in the swimming pool, where he would develop the skills that would give him his first real taste of success.

But south-east London definitely also played an important part in Jason's formative years. At some point as a teenager he lived in Sydenham, south of Camberwell and Dulwich, while training as a diver at the nearby Crystal Palace National Sports Centre. The area was clearly close to his heart and he felt at home there: years later, in the mid-to-late 1990s, he would live in Sydenham with his beautiful girlfriend, the model Kelly Brook.

Born to a market tradesman and a seamstress, Jason has been keen to protect his and his family's right to privacy. He has avoided revealing too much about his past – defending intrusive questions with guile and grace – and he remains protective of those closest to him. When he was interviewed by the US chat-show host Jay Leno in 2010, he talked briefly and humourously about his south-east London background. 'Was it a tough area?' asked Leno. 'Yeah,' replied Jason, 'they weren't exactly playing croquet and quaffing champagne at weekends … yeah, it's near Brixton, pretty tough down there.'

Given that he has been so guarded about his past, and defensive of those closest to him, very little is known about Jason's parents or his older brother. He has regularly been described in profiles as the 'second son of a lounge singer and dressmaker-turned-dancer' but his family's working life was less glamorous than this sounded.

Utilising the charm and charisma that his son would develop on screen, Jason's father spent his time running the family business. During interviews over the years Jason has confirmed that his father worked on Yarmouth market, and that he either ran a bathroom stall or sold silver-plated trays, hi-fis, cameras, glassware and china – 'liquidation goods', as he once called them – on Sunday mornings.

In his own words, 'My father used to work in mock auctions, it's sort of like a contest with prizes and big TVs. And I used to work in the back room, carrying things out. We had a shop on the east coast of England, which was governed by five or six of these mock auctions. When I was on summer vacation from school, I used to work in these shops with my dad and his friends, learning the ropes. When I left

21

school I was working on the streets myself, selling jewellery and perfume.'

'Mock auctions' involved selling cheap, low-quality goods at inflated prices. The organisers would aim to attract a street audience, wind them up into a buying frenzy and get them to buy over-priced goods in the belief that they were, in fact, bargains. They would achieve this through clever marketing and by initially getting friends in the crowd to be seen purchasing higher-value goods at lower prices. A Westminster Council warning about mock auctions in 2006 noted that the 'enthusiasm to bid is whipped up by a man with a microphone and an auctioneer's hammer'.

It's not hard to imagine the impact these early adventures in this working world might have had on the young Jason. Clearly it's where he first developed the gift of the gab and found the courage and confidence to express himself in a charming way. 'It's street theatre,' he'd explain. 'You have to make it entertaining so people don't get bored and walk away.'

The business played a big part in family life. Jason's brother worked on the market and even Jason, when he wasn't at school, was pitching in, helping out in the shops and on the stalls, picking up tips from his father.

It isn't difficult to see where Jason got his hustler instinct from. Weekends and holidays spent traipsing around after his father and working in the shop must have taught him all he needed to know about the art of selling. More than that, it must have instilled in him a real sense of self-made fortune.

But it wasn't just theatrical salesman skills that the family passed on to him. His parents were very musical and were also fond of ballroom dancing. Jason once told the *New York*

Times that he had played drums in his family's band with his brother on guitar and his father as lead singer. We also know that his parents later moved to the Canary Islands after Jason became successful and that his father began performing in a Sinatra-style cabaret act, ably assisted by Jason's mother. 'She's a dancer, my dad's a singer now,' Jason said. 'So they do this little double-act. They're quite the couple. Tom Jones gets all the skimpy panties thrown at him when he sings, my dad gets the big apple-catcher underwear tossed on stage.'

But that's as far as Jason would ever go in conversations about his family. Admirably, he's always been cautious about revealing too much. We only know that his family has been vital in supporting him on his extraordinary journey towards Hollywood fame. 'My family's great, like a rock to me,' he once said. 'I think it's very important to keep in touch with people that mean a lot to you. It just seems like the time that I do get off, it is so important for me to go back and see my folks and friends.'

At the height of his early success – when his second film *Snatch* came out in 2000 – Jason was asked what his parents and friends thought of his new career. He confirmed that, understandably, they had been extremely supportive of his work. He reveals, 'You know, they think "Good on ya! Do as much as you can with it!" My parents are proud, obviously. Sometimes I have to pinch myself every time I'm in another film. It's bizarre.' Not coming from a 'starry' background has meant that Jason has always been able to keep in touch with the value systems of the world in which he grew up. That said, the rewards of film stardom and the trappings of fame have obviously affected the lives of those closest to him. In 2009, for example, it was reported that Jason's parents were flying out to be with him at Planet Hollywood in Las Vegas to celebrate his father's birthday. This was hardly the most ostentatious statement for the family to make, but it was nevertheless very different to – if not necessarily better than – beers and curry in Great Yarmouth.

Although Jason would never train to be an actor – performing with the family band seems to be the only early indication of any hunger or craving for the limelight – his passion for films had always been there. 'Well, as a kid, everyone wants to be in a film, but really it just came out of the blue,' he once said. 'It's something I never dreamed I'd be doing, making movies.'

Perhaps surprisingly, in his early years he was fond of musicals like *On the Town* and actors and dancers such as Gene Kelly and Donald O'Connor. 'I used to watch musicals all the time when I was a kid. I love *Singing in the Rain* and *Seven Brides for Seven Brothers*, *West Side Story*. I grew up on them. My mum and dad were fanatics on musicals. I don't think they work now, although the romantic comedy side of me hasn't been exposed.'

Indeed, Jason's working life would take quite a different path: despite this early fondness for song, dance and romance, his film career suggests he was primarily inspired by somewhat darker genres. Talking of this he admitted, 'I actually never thought I'd get involved in action movies', but growing up, he devoured tough-guy adventure films featuring his favourite actors; stars such as Kirk Douglas, Paul Newman, Steve McQueen, Charles Bronson and Clint Eastwood. 'Kirk Douglas in *Spartacus* was my man when growing up,' he once said. 'I like Clint Eastwood, all those guys are the people that are in the movies I watch time and again:

Cool Hand Luke and *Butch Cassidy and the Sundance Kid.* They're the movies that I've been inspired by since I was a kid. People like movies for different reasons and I just think these are the kind of actors that both the girls and guys like. They've just got universal appeal.'

They were filmstars who, either consciously or subconsciously, would have an impact on his own style of dramatic performance. Film directors who have worked with him over the years have compared his vocal delivery with that of Clint Eastwood, noted similarities with Paul Newman in his understated performances, or identified parallels in his all-action style with the acting of Steve McQueen.

Another key film influence on the young Jason would be the James Bond films. 'Growing up, I was the biggest Bond fan,' he once said, and – as rumour would have it – when Daniel Craig took over from Pierce Brosnan as 007, Jason Statham was also on the (very) shortlist. Perhaps, as some critics have speculated, he will be the man to step into Craig's shoes during the next decade. After all, in 2010 he achieved another of his childhood ambitions by working on a movie (*The Expendables*) with one of his heroes, Sylvester Stallone: 'I've been watching his films for years, yes, I watched all the *Rocky* films as a kid growing up in England, so I'm very familiar with everything he's done. That's why I get excited when I get to do a film like this.'

If the young Jason ever really did believe he could have a career in films, then the most likely route would have been as a stuntman. When he was living in South London he was aware of Camberwell's famous Powell family, who had performed stunts in James Bond films for over forty years. Fred 'Nosher' Powell and his brother Dennis 'Dinny' Powell were two of the most sought-after fall-guys in Hollywood and had stood in for Sean Connery and Roger Moore respectively.

Nosher's eldest son Greg had been a stuntman for Roger Moore and Timothy Dalton, while Greg's brother Gary doubled for Pierce Brosnan before working with Daniel Craig. (Gary, playing Brosnan, famously flipped the speedboat in *The World is Not Enough* and also choreographed the car chase in *Quantum of Solace*. His girlfriend, Nikki Berwick, did the stunts for Bond girl Olga Kurylenko in . . . *Solace*.)

'A lot of the main stuntmen are English,' Jason once told Simon Lewis of the *Daily Mail*. 'Nosher and his sons are big noises in America. You need at least six disciplines to get on the Stunt Register: horse-riding, driving, martial arts, high falls, swimming, gymnastics . . . I think I had about four of the six disciplines but the other two would have meant serious hard work away from the diving pool so I never had the time.'

CHAPTER TWO:

TEENAGE DREAMS

As a teenager, Jason Statham wasn't exactly the shy and retiring type. He has described himself as 'rebellious' and as a 'streetwise kid'. However, rather than getting into too much trouble, his saving grace would be a passion for sport. He played football for his school team and has always loved the game. This would be clear from his enjoyable performance as the mad Scottish goalkeeper Monk in *Mean Machine*. Later in his film career, once he had relocated to Los Angeles, he would also appear regularly for a Hollywood all-star team featuring his friend Vinnie Jones – Jason's co-star in *Lock Stock . . .* , *Snatch* and *Mean Machine* – and Steve Jones of the Sex Pistols. Unfortunately, Jason would have to give up playing for fear that injuries would damage his action man film career.

But the young Jason was an all-round athlete, into gymnastics and activities such as trampolining and the high jump.

He also played a lot of racquet sports, such as tennis and squash. Before he got heavily into swimming and diving, additional stuntman disciplines he would learn included boxing and martial arts. He has always been a big fan of boxing and it seems that this enthusiasm was encouraged by his father – who had been both a boxer and a gymnast – and by his older brother, who trained in martial arts. One of Jason's school friends in Great Yarmouth was the heavy-weight boxer Scott Welch, who claimed five boxing titles in a seven-year career, before going on to appear alongside Jason in Guy Ritchie's *Snatch*, where he helped choreograph the fist fights with Brad Pitt.

But it seems as if Jason was always more into martial arts than pugilism. Years later he would reflect, 'I used to do a lot of kick-boxing. My dad used to box. I do a lot of grappling now and, you know, the movie martial arts.' Aside from his brother's influence, his interest in martial arts was really inspired by the great combat films of the 1970s and 1980s and by actors such as Jet Li, Jackie Chan and Bruce Lee.

Of these three heroes, Bruce Lee died long before Jason was aware of the great kung fu fighter's extraordinary career, but his legacy – films such as *Fist of Fury*, *The Way of the Dragon* and *Enter the Dragon* – continued to have a huge impact on British audiences. Although Bruce Lee died of a cerebral edema on 20 June 1973, aged only thirty-two, he had developed his own style of mixed martial arts called jeet kune do ('the way of the intercepting fist') by refining his knowledge of diverse disciplines such as wing chun and incorporating elements such as traditional boxing and Okinawan karate.

Having opened his own kung fu studios in Los Angeles, Bruce Lee also provided personal martial arts training for Steve McQueen and James Coburn. (Bruce Lee's son Brandon Lee was killed in a freak accident on the set of the cult film *The Crow*. On several occasions Jason has expressed interest in remaking *The Crow* and playing Brandon's role.)

Another popular culture figure whose martial arts work would have an influence on the young Jason was David Carradine in the popular television series *Kung Fu*. Carradine starred as the philosophical fighting Buddhist monk who, in the defensive style of The Transporter, Frank Martin, walked in peace and reluctantly always outfought the villains. Carradine and his career would also have an impact on Jason's life in films. Having starred in the 1975 film *Death Race 2000*, he'd return as the voice of Frankenstein in Paul W. S. Anderson's 2008 remake, the title of which was abbreviated to *Death Race*. Plus, Carradine would also appear alongside Jason in *Crank 2: High Voltage* as the veteran triad boss, Poon Dog.

But, if it ever looked as if Jason's sports career would focus mainly on football or athletics or boxing or martial arts, things changed for him at around the age of thirteen or fourteen. 'I was on holiday with the parents, years and years ago,' he later recalled, 'and I saw some guy do a high dive and I said, "You know what, let me have a go at that." It was just this stupid idea that I'd be able to do it.'

Whereas most potential world-class divers started training at the age of four or five years old – particularly in the leading competitive diving nations such as Russia and China – Jason only began to dive seriously from the age of fifteen. He started getting up before dawn every morning, training from

5:30 to 7:00 a.m. every morning before school, then returning to practise in the pool each evening.

Hoping to be the Tom Daley of his day, by the mid-1980s Jason seems to have left school, moved to Sydenham near the Crystal Palace National Sports Centre, and started practising daily with Daniel T. Johnson to perfect his diving techniques: 'We used to compete on a ten-metre platform and a three-metre springboard, which is not necessarily very high, but we used to do a certain amount of gymnastic tricks off there. We'd do backwards three-and-a-halves. You know, like [Olympic-winning American diver] Greg Louganis.' At one point in his diving career, Jason was coached by Kim White, who also worked at Southend Diving Club and went on to become British Diving Programme Manager.

Ever his own harshest critic, Jason would go on to express disappointment with his achievements as a diver – 'I was trying to win an Olympic gold medal' – but by most people's standards he was very successful indeed. Clearly, training to the absolute peak of physical fitness, and performing at the highest level of international athletic competition, would contribute hugely to his later success. It helped give him the drive and determination that has made Jason the major action star he is today. For over a decade he was one of the best divers in the British team, finishing third in Olympic trials on three different occasions and achieving twelfth-place in the World Championships of 1992.

He also competed in the Commonwealth Games in 1990. Although he didn't win a medal, an Edinburgh Diving Club report on the efforts of their own swimmer Steve Forrest at the games (held in New Zealand) confirmed Jason's sig-nificant ranking in the sport: 'Steve dived well in the platform event, finishing ahead of Tony Ally and Jason Statham, who were England's leading lights.'

Even though he had started diving relatively late in life, through achieving so much in the sport Jason proved to himself and to others that he had incredible focus, fitness and self-belief. These would all prove to be important factors in the years to come.

Regardless of his lack of major medals, and although he would occasionally under-value or speak modestly of the years he had committed to the sport – 'I did it for a while, it was just a silly hobby' – clearly the diving life had plenty of other, extra-curricular rewards. Apart from maintaining his high level of physical fitness, he also travelled extensively and, apparently, played as hard as he trained. 'I ran round the world competing,' Jason told Simon Lewis of the *Daily Mail*. 'It took me to Germany, France, Italy, Russia, Australia, you name it. It's a big circuit, and if you're competing for your country, you get all the perks. Like jumping into bed with all the opposing teams' females . . . it's a race to get them drunk at the banquet.'

He also joked about his 'ladies' man' reputation in an interview with *The Times* newspaper's Chrissy Iley, amusingly suggesting that his entire sporting career had been prompted by one classic television commercial: 'All I ever wanted to do was the Milk Tray advert, where the guy comes in, delivers the chocolates, jumps off a cliff and dives in. That Milk Tray advert is the reason I got into diving, although these days I'd be hanging around in a wardrobe waiting for her to be in bed, sneak in, slip under the sheets, fuck the chocolates.'

Later still, offering another fascinating insight into his character as both an athlete and a film star, he also talked about the high (diving) life to the *Los Angeles Times*: 'I was on the British team travelling around the world with a British tracksuit on and jumping in bed with Russian girls. It was a little hobby that ended up taking out ten years of my life. I was never as dedicated as I should have been. I had spurts of dedication. Feast or famine. That's all I am. The middle is boring. If you're going to do something, do it with style! Get amongst it! Whatever you do, do it to the extreme.'

Those who had imagined competitive aquatics to be a totally fun-free, hard-training, physically-exhausting, body-building, gruelling business might reflect on the case of Mike Fibbens, one of Jason's national colleagues, and a British champion who was banned for two years, later reduced to one, for cocaine abuse. A well-known figure in London's clubland, Fibbens also trained hard but played harder. 'World swimming looked no further than him for a party,' wrote the *Independent* in a July 2000 article, after Fibbens' drugs ban had been confirmed. 'The world of Mike Fibbens is a world of models, film stars and, believe it or not, swimming. Kate Moss, the cast of *Lock Stock & Two Smoking Barrels* and Bill Wyman are as much a part of his week as the children he swims with in Swiss Cottage, London.'

In the interview, Fibbens also talked about his friendships in the world of sporting celebrity: 'I've known Jason Statham for over ten years from his days on the national diving team and, after starring as one of the leads in *Lock Stock* . . . , the cast he brought with him were the hottest bookings in town when the film took off.'

Jason, thankfully, managed to avoid any of the major pitfalls associated with the darker elements of high-level sport. He probably didn't realise it at the time, but later he could point to many positive and lasting benefits from his diving career, both physically and mentally. 'It was a great experience, you know, to travel the world and compete at a certain level. It teaches you discipline, focus and certainly keeps you out of trouble.' Obviously, these hard-learned abilities would play a major part in the next stage of his life.

By the mid-1990s, Jason's time as a competitive diver was coming to an end when the national squad relocated from Crystal Palace to new facilities in Sheffield. Although he was probably uncertain about his future career, there suddenly seemed to be a lot more stability in his domestic world. Most importantly, in 1996 on an early modelling assignment in Greece, he had met one of the greatest loves of his life, the gorgeous seventeen-year-old Kelly Brook (then known as Kelly Parsons), who would go on to become a model pin-up, national heart-throb, *Big Breakfast* television presenter and, later, film star.

Although Jason would never say much about this first meeting, or their much-discussed relationship, in 2000 Kelly told Frank Skinner about the beginning of their romance. 'He was a diver, a high-board diver before I met him and he was in the Commonwealth Games. We met in Santorini in Greece. He was on a modelling shoot and so was I. He'd just been spotted and we were both out there doing a shoot. We had some mutual friends out there. So I kind of knew him before he was in *Lock Stock* . . . and he knew me before I did *The Big Breakfast*. So it was nice to get together before all that happened. We've got a nice house now and it's all lovely.'

When she first really got to know Jason in South London – he was in Sydenham and she was living with her parents in Rochester, Kent – he was apparently still working on the markets, driving an old blue van. That Jason would have once had to rely on such a modest form of transport is difficult to imagine today, given that the young man in the driving seat would become one of the cinema world's most respected stunt drivers. He would even star in Audi's famous A3 TDI 'progress is beautiful' commercial, screened in the largest audience-grabbing commercial television slot on the planet during American Football's Superbowl 2009.

More astonishing still, perhaps, while talking to Jay Leno in 2010, Jason revealed that he had struggled with driving lessons and failed to pass his test: 'I used to get into a lot of bad habits. I'd drive my dad's van, years ago, when I was fifteen. He'd get tired and I'd take over and it's hard to get out of bad habits. It was the driving I failed the test on. I failed it two or three times. I'd drive to the test, fail and drive home.'

'What were you doing wrong in the actual test?' asked the incredulous Leno.

'Everything,' laughed Jason. 'You're driving too close, you're on the phone, you're smoking a cigar.'

Following in the footsteps of his father and his older brother, the ducking-and-diving arts of street trading (or 'street theatre', as he would often call it) played a large part in Jason's early life. After leaving school, he had had to fund his amateur diving by raising money as and when he could. It wasn't always legitimate but it seemed to fit in with his nomadic lifestyle and, frankly, it was the working world he had grown to know and love.

Once Jason had moved on from street hustling to film stardom – the two would forever be intricately connected in his success story – he would always look back on his street life with openness, warmth and affection. 'I used to put money in my pocket while working on the street corners, selling perfume and jewellery, and other goods that were supposedly expensive,' he'd tell interviewers. 'Street-corner sales, on the fly. You open up your case, and when the police come you close up. It's kind of illegal. That's why you work with look-outs and several stooges in the crowd.'

Jason would, of course, play a character that wasn't too far from his experience in the opening scenes of his first Guy Ritchie film, *Lock Stock & Two Smoking Barrels*, even using some of his own tried-and-tested sales lines in the process, notably 'handmade in Italy, hand-stolen in Stepney'. American interviewers, Jay Leno in particular, would later sound slightly horrified but deeply fascinated by this un-orthodox background.

'Did this stuff happen to fall off the back of a lorry, Jason?' asked Jay Leno.

'They didn't fall off the back of a lorry, Jay,' he replied. 'Somebody pushed them and I caught them! It was very lucrative ... we made thousands of pounds. You didn't have to pay a lot of tax. It was called fly pitching. You work with a team, people in the crowd, guys who stand look-out for the police.'

Monica Corcoran of the *New York Times* observed, 'It's not hard to imagine Mr Statham as a successful salesman. He smiles wide and winks often and periodically announces "My name is Billy, not silly" to comic effect.'

Although Jason would assure interviewers that he had never been to prison or had a criminal record, he told the two female presenters on NBC's *Today Show* exactly where and how his business worked: 'It's something I learnt as a kid. My dad was doing the same thing, my brother did the same thing. It's just the family business. I was working Argyle Street, which is off London's Oxford Street. Knightsbridge, outside Harrods. Any of the places that was very busy for shoppers ... Yeah, I used to sell fake perfume and jewellery on street corners. Did I tell people they were fake? Absolutely not ... I was hustling.'

Later, when asked how he was coping with his movie-star fame, one of the NBC presenters suggested, 'I bet you couldn't walk down Oxford Street today without getting mobbed'. To which Jason laughed and responded, 'Yeah, they're all looking for their money back from the jewellery I used to sell!'

It wasn't really surprising, in the same television interview, when one of the presenters flirtatiously said to him, 'Swimmers have the best bodies ... that's my personal opinion.' If the family business of street trading and street-corner sales had been a necessary cash-raising venture during his diving years, soon there would be new, very different, professional opportunities on the horizon. Although he'd categorically state, 'I've never been one to run around in Speedos on the beach', by his early-to-mid twenties Jason had developed an extraordinary physique to go with his rugged good looks, playful sense of humour and natural charisma. How else could he have captured the much-coveted heart of Kelly Brook?

Given Jason's hugely competitive drive, it would not be long before he would develop another successful – and lucrative – line of business. In the early-to-mid-1990s, while training on the diving board at Crystal Palace, he had been spotted by a modelling agency that specialised in athletes.

Initially he had been offered work showcasing sportswear, but he was soon being pursued as a new talent in wider commercials and print campaigns. Early lucrative contracts included modelling for Tommy Hilfiger, Levi Strauss & Co. and on the catwalk for Griffin menswear (for their 1996 spring/summer catalogue).

But Jason certainly wasn't being marketed as a typical pretty-boy; his appeal as a model was intended to be unorthodox, emphasising the working-class, man-in-the-street elements of his character. As the *LA Times* would retrospectively observe, 'He had a brief career as a fashion model, but even then his poses had an air of menace.'

There would be some small-screen work too, including very brief appearances in the Beautiful South's 'Dream a Little Dream' and as a male model in Erasure's 'Run to the Sun' in 1994. He would later star as The Transporter in the 2008 promo for rapper Knoc-turn'al's 'Muzik'.

The most memorable of all Jason's British advertising appearances would come when he was signed up by Kit Kat for their famous, simply shot and brilliantly scripted 'break philosopher' commercial – 'The Salmon'.

Cue Jason, sitting in a South London café, with a mug of tea and his favourite four-fingered chocolate biscuit: 'The salmon spends its life relentlessly striving to get upstream ... with ceaseless endeavour it rides the currents of massive rivers ... drags itself over rocks and shallow water ... forces its way up huge waterfalls. Never stops ... never rests. Just battles and battles its way upstream. Finally ... heroically, it reaches its goal ... and it's absolutely knackered ... Then it dies ... Remember ... you are not a salmon.'

With the traditional pay-off line 'Have a break, have a Kit

Kat' – one of the strongest and most enduring slogans in British advertising – Jason's performance received great praise and recognition, particularly within the advertising industry. It even inspired a self-congratulatory passage from the advert's creators in their presentation for the APG, the authority in Advertising and Communications Strategy. In their report they declared, 'The creative idea we fell in love with we call "Break Philosophers" – an explosion of analogies, stories, facts and illustrations, each pointing out how important breaks are.'

Jason was thought to be the perfect face for the promotional campaign. 'With a strong, credible spokesperson in Jason Statham, some hard-hitting press and the sad tale of a fish who never took a break, we launched a campaign that is destined to capture the relieved imaginations of a hard-working population and give them nuggets of inspiration to encourage them to reconsider their breaking habits. "You are not a salmon" entered the vernacular (every time one of us hears it, in the back of a cab, in a pub, amongst a group of kids on the bus, we are reminded that we were onto something in the first place, which is something of a relief for us).'

The advert was a huge success and had something akin to a cult following. The APG report concluded: 'The response of consumers has been breathtaking, ranging from one viewer nominating Kit Kat for a Nobel Peace Prize, to the slightly more substantial evidence of record-breaking tracking results and, most pleasing of all, an uplift in full-value sales of the brand.'

The Kit Kat contract may have been Jason's most lucrative and well-known work as a small-screen model, but another assignment would have a far greater impact on his career. In 1997, he was hired to do some magazine modelling for the European clothing retailer French Connection. During a break from work, Jason was introduced to one of the French Connection bosses, Stephen Marks, who also turned out to be a major investor in a forthcoming British film being made by a young director called Guy Ritchie. The film would be called *Lock Stock & Two Smoking Barrels*, and – Jason was told – Ritchie was looking to cast authentic London faces in supporting roles.

This would turn out to be a life-changing moment for Jason. If, deep down, he really believed that he had never fulfilled his true potential as an international diver, then perhaps this sense of failure had given him the hunger, the drive and the determination to make a name for himself in a new arena. Jason would audition for Guy Ritchie, grasp the opportunity with both hands, and never look back.

CHAPTER THREE:

LOCK STOCK &
TWO SMOKING BARRELS

Before the early 2000s, before he became *more* famous for being the husband of Madonna, Guy Ritchie helped revitalise British cinema. In the mid-to-late 1990s he emerged as a mover and shaker who was reluctant to accept that the film industry was on its knees and destined to stay in the shadows of Hollywood. As a director and writer he had strong visual ideas, black humour, sharp dialogue and original thinking. Most importantly, Ritchie and his SKA Films producer/partner Matthew Vaughn seemed to have the energy and drive to cut through red tape, sidestep cynicism, raise funding and make things happen. They wouldn't accept 'No' for an answer.

Although he had only made one film before – a 1995 short called *The Hard Case* – Guy Ritchie would prove himself to be a real maverick with his first feature, *Lock Stock & Two Smoking Barrels*. Fired by his love of British gangster films,

TV cop shows and crime thrillers, and undoubtedly inspired by the youthful successes of Quentin Tarantino (*Reservoir Dogs* and *Pulp Fiction*) and Danny Boyle (*Shallow Grave* and *Trainspotting*), Ritchie set out to shoot a gritty, dark comedy; a violent yet affectionate portrait of the London underworld.

Above all, Guy Ritchie wanted the film to be both entertaining and realistic. In order to do this, he set out to recruit an ensemble cast of London characters; some with acting experience, but most blessed with lived-in working-class faces that wouldn't look out of place on an identity parade.

'When you're making a film set in this very gritty world,' Ritchie explained, 'you need the audience to believe that these people aren't just a bunch of posh actors dressed up as gangsters, boxers and petty thieves. You have to believe it's real. I try to pepper that world with locations and extras that are as authentic as possible.'

'Guy's obsessed with making sure there's credibility to it,' confirmed producer Matthew Vaughn. 'The bad guys really look bad . . . he's steered clear of some of the character actors we have in Britain and gone for the real McCoys . . . we've got some real-life villains in the film, which does make it unique.'

Hardly a 'real-life villain', clearly Jason Statham was born to feature in *Lock Stock & Two Smoking Barrels*. The 'street theatre' world of his hustling conman youth would prove to be perfect training for his role in Ritchie's film: 'All of a sudden I met with Guy Ritchie and he had written a script about this bunch of London lads and one of them was this street-corner conman, and I was the authentic person to play it.' Who else would better know the language, the lifestyle and the etiquettes that rule that world. 'You know, I had lived that lifestyle and I knew all about the dialogue that these people use, and so rather than use an actor he used the real thing. So that was my first attempt at acting.'

The unusual story of Jason Statham's audition for *Lock Stock & Two Smoking Barrels* has become legendary in the film world. It's a classic case of someone being in the right place at the right time; of someone grabbing the chance of a lifetime with both hands and, in Jason's case, literally not letting go.

His international diving career was coming to an end and, by his own confession, he had been funding his lifestyle using his charms as black-market salesman to sell jewellery on Argyll Street near London's Oxford Circus. But, more importantly, he'd also started doing some modelling work for the clothing firm French Connection. It transpired that one of the French Connection bosses was involved in a forthcoming new British film, the debut feature by a young director called Guy Ritchie.

'It was a combination of me knowing someone that he knew,' recalled Jason, 'and the meeting was set. I told him about my past and he thought I would bring an authenticity to the role.'

At the actual audition, Guy Ritchie told Jason he could have the role of Bacon – one of four central characters engaged in a risky get-rich-quick scheme to repay a massive gambling debt – if he could convince Ritchie to buy some fake jewellery. Through his family background working the street markets and auctions, Jason had developed the gift of the gab; the rare ability to convince punters that they were getting a brilliant bargain; to seduce them into buying things they really didn't want or need. By the end of the audition, legend has it, Guy had bought four pieces of jewellery and

Jason had his first acting role in the bag. Importantly, like a true salesman, Jason allegedly left the audition without returning Ritchie's cash.

Years later, Jason would understandably look back on this life-changing moment with great warmth and good humour: 'He was casting people from the street, looking for fresh faces ... A good friend of mine, Vinnie Jones, was an ex-soccer player, he got in the movie. Then Lenny McLean* was a boxer ... Guy was just looking for interesting authentic-type guys.'

It wasn't as if Jason had spent his youth going to drama school and playing Joseph in the school nativity. As Jason recalls, 'I kind of ... fell into it. Somebody put me in a room with Guy and he decided to give me a part in a movie, so it's not like I had a burning desire to be an actor. Guy thinks going to drama school is the worst thing in the world. It all just happened by accident ... just one of those lucky right-time-and-right-place moments.'

A decade later, in a 2008 interview with the *Los Angeles Times* – in the era of his Hollywood successes with *Transporter 3* and *The Bank Job* – Jason again looked back affectionately to the day he convinced Guy Ritchie he was the right man: 'There were two reasons. He wanted to save some money, and he wanted street credibility. Guy shovelled me up off the street. Without him there wouldn't be all this.'

If you study cinema, if you read the classic text-books on the art of cinematic storytelling, or attend film or screen-

---

* McLean died before *Lock Stock* ... was released, so Ritchie dedicated the film to his memory. The 'unlicensed' heavyweight boxing champion of the world had been an 'authentic' former associate of the Kray twins.

writing courses, much emphasis is placed on the importance of visually introducing central characters to the audience. Their first few frames on screen should endeavour to establish who they are and what they might contribute to the story.

The opening images, the opening words of *Lock Stock & Two Smoking Barrels*, belonged to Jason Statham. Perfectly cast as Bacon – the shaven-headed South London street hustler, dressed in a donkey jacket with a tartan scarf, selling knock-off jewellery and dodgy handbags – he's underneath the arches, in the back streets, standing in front of some corrugated iron locked-up shop: 'Right . . . let's sort the buyers from the spy-ers, the needy from the greedy, and those who trust me from the ones who don't . . .'

If the scripted lines were Guy Ritchie's then the delivery, the street poetry, was one hundred per cent Jason. It's part music hall, part sexual innuendo, part menacing bouncer, part loveable rogue, part *Carry On*: 'Take a bag . . . I took a bag home last night . . . cost me a lot more than ten pounds, I can tell you.' It was a funny, edgy, uncomfortable, realistic scene that perfectly set the tone for *Lock Stock & Two Smoking Barrels*. As soon as Bacon mutters the couplet, 'too late too late will be the cry, when the man with the bargains has passed you by', the police – a.k.a. the 'rozzers', the 'pigs', the 'filth' – are upon them, like Keystone Cops chasing Ritchie's rogues through the mean streets of East London.

But if the introductory scenes presented small-time crooks struggling to make a dishonest living, the core of Ritchie's idea was to propel these attractively hopeless lowlifes into the heavy-duty world of serious organised crime.

The plot – simplistically described in the movie trailer as

'four friends with a money-making scheme that's quick ... easy ... and *very* expensive' – focused on card-sharp Eddie (Nick Moran) and his three mates Bacon (Jason Statham), Fat Man a.k.a. Tom (Jason Flemyng) and Soap (Dexter Fletcher). Looking to make some fast cash, they inevitably got into deep trouble, way over their heads, and found themselves owing £500,000 to Harry 'Porn King' Lansdale. Unless they paid it back within one week, the gang will have their fingers slowly, painfully separated from their bodies by McLean's Barry the Baptist (he drowned people who failed to pay their debts).

With the sales-pitch tag-line 'A disgrace to criminals everywhere', *Lock Stock & Two Smoking Barrels* was set in a sleazy man's world of three-card brag games in boxing rings, stolen antiques, pub violence, hard drinking, drug deals and robbery with violence. Unusually (given the '18' certificate), the movie was sex-free; in fact, there's only one real female role.

Ritchie's script was tongue-in-cheek, riddled with rhyming slang, Anglo-Saxon oaths and great one-liners, but the film had a terrific pace, tension and excitement to it; sparkling cinema, cleverly directed; fast cuts, big close-ups and almost balletic use of slow motion. For example, the scene in which Eddie loses the card game was beautifully realised. He staggers from the boxing ring like a shattered, punch-drunk prizefighter; visually it was a cross between a scene from Gus Van Zandt's *Drugstore Cowboy* and a lavishly shot vodka commercial.

The supporting cast of *Lock Stock* ... was also strong, including fine cameos from Sting (as Eddie's dad) and Rob Bryden (as an unfortunate traffic warden) plus a fantastic comedy performance from Vas Blackwood as the Blaxploitation-spoof bad guy Mr Breaker.

Even in this company Jason Statham shone in every scene. He might not have come across as a Hollywood-action-heroin-waiting – despite the acrobatic backward somersault from a standing position in one bar-room scene – and he certainly couldn't compete with the crazed menace of Vinnie Jones as Big Chris, but for an untrained debutant he revealed tremendous screen presence. If, as a child, he'd admired the McQueens and Newmans and Eastwoods because they appealed to both men and women, then as an adult taking his first steps as an apprentice film actor, he didn't have to try too hard to appear naturally charismatic on camera – even in a big brown leather coat.

Guy Ritchie, a fan of the gangster genre, had clearly done his homework: there were elements of classic American mob movies in the make-up of *Lock Stock & Two Smoking Barrels*. Everything from *The French Connection*, *The Godfather*, and *Carlito's Way* through to *Goodfellas* seemed to have informed his cinematic vision; inevitably there was a reference to *Scarface* in the dialogue. Despite the influence of Tarantino's directing techniques, plus a fast-cutting visual style more familiar in expensive pop promos and classy car adverts, the film aimed to be firmly in the tradition of great British crime capers.

The obvious comparisons would be 1980 Docklands chiller *The Long Good Friday* starring Bob Hoskins and the Peter Medak-directed *The Krays* (1990) featuring those Spandau Ballet brothers (Gary and Martin Kemp) in conflict with rival ganglord Steven Berkoff; dark films but with elements of Ealing-style black humour reminiscent of *The Lavender Hill*

Mob (1951) or *Kind Hearts and Coronets* (1949), or even the iconoclastic 1960s plays of Joe Orton. Plus, obviously, *Lock Stock ...* contained plenty of territorial and linguistic references of grainy, leathery, violently comedic London TV crime shows such as *The Sweeney* and *Minder*.

But there were also shades of earlier realistic British underworld thrillers in Ritchie's work, notably the film version of *Brighton Rock* (1947) featuring Richard Attenborough as psychotic Pinkie Brown, *Get Carter* (1971) with Michael Caine as the violent Kray-era London gangster on Tyneside wreaking murderous revenge on his brother's killers, and even *Villain* (also 1971) with Richard Burton playing a Ronnie Kray-style sadistic gay gangster who's kind to his mother but cruel to everyone else. (*Villain* was scripted by Dick Clement and Ian La Frenais, creators of *The Likely Lads*, *Porridge* and *Auf Wiedersehen, Pet*. Jason Statham would star in their 2008 film, *The Bank Job*.)

Arguably, without the crime genre successes of *Lock Stock & Two Smoking Barrels* and Antonia Bird's *Face* (1997), the trio of year 2000 gangland thrillers – *Love, Honour and Obey*, *Essex Boys* and the excellent *Sexy Beast* – would have received less exposure.

Unsurprisingly, the reviews for *Lock Stock & Two Smoking Barrels* were incredibly positive. *The Sun* described it as 'the number one film of 1998, one of the most entertaining movies ever made'; the *Daily Star* hailed it as 'the best British crime caper in years ... slick, funny ... see it!'; and even the broadsheets celebrated Guy Ritchie's film. For *The Guardian*, it was 'slick, upbeat, pounding, brilliant!'

Various annual awards ceremonies in late 1998 and 1999 also recognised Guy Ritchie's film and celebrated his original talent. *Lock Stock* ... was named 'Best British Film' at the Empire Awards and also won trophies at the British Comedy Awards, the Tokyo International Film Festival, the British Independent Film Awards, the MTV Movie Awards and the *Evening Standard* Film Awards.

Although few film reviewers mentioned Jason Statham in despatches, his street-hustler-to-film-star tale was one of the real success stories. The other three actors featured in the movie's central quartet – Jason Flemyng (*Lovejoy*, *Rob Roy*, *Spice World*), Nick Moran (*The Bill*, *Grange Hill*, *Eldorado*) and Dexter Fletcher (*Press Gang*, *The Long Good Friday*, *Bugsy Malone*) – all had previous TV or screen credits to their names. In total contrast, Jason Statham had come from nowhere. He wouldn't be going back.

His life was changed by *Lock Stock & Two Smoking Barrels*. Aside from media interest in his rags-to-relative-riches story, he had formed a close bond with film director Guy Ritchie. 'I love that man, he's so talented,' he'd later remark. 'He's a man with vision ... every time I get to see him I'm as happy as a pig in shit.' Thanks to Guy Ritchie, Jason had a new career as a film actor and, through Ritchie's rapidly expanding contact book of Hollywood connections, Jason and his glamour-girl teenage girlfriend Kelly Brook would start to move in very different social, A-list celebrity circles.

Guy Ritchie's personal life had also been dramatically transformed during the *Lock Stock* ... production. The film's cast had included Sting, and – even more significantly – the Police frontman's wife Trudie Styler, was one of the executive producers. Through Sting and Styler, Ritchie was introduced in 1998 to Madonna, who agreed to release the *Lock Stock* ...

soundtrack on her label, Maverick*. Their love affair, which was followed by marriage in December 2000, had started to develop from there.

Bolstered by the commercial and critical successes of *Lock Stock & Two Smoking Barrels* (which also led to a spin-off TV series), and now with major-league celebrity backing from Madonna and her US film industry contacts, Guy Ritchie, Matthew Vaughn and the SKA team focused on their second feature film. Whereas *Lock Stock . . .* had initially struggled for British film distribution, the follow-up was almost guaranteed to secure the international backing it needed.

According to Vaughn, Guy Ritchie had been writing the script for *Diamonds* – it would eventually be called *Snatch* – before *Lock Stock . . .* had even been released: 'He was still living and breathing the genre of hard-men characters. It took us a long time to find the right faces – we had to see hundreds . . . Guy has such strong visual references that he wanted people not only to look the part but to deliver maximum authenticity with minimum theatrical technique.'

'What started as a blood-rich thriller ended up on set as a gangster comedy of errors,' explained Ritchie. 'It's fast-paced, "move-it-quick" and with no fat on it. I also love playing around with dialogue . . . so this film has some of the material I wanted to put in my first film but couldn't get in.'

This time, Ritchie and Vaughn looked beyond the usual suspects and battered faces of the London underworld. The

* Stylish use of music played a major part in the success of Ritchie's movies. The *Lock Stock . . .* mix memorably featured Pete Wingfield and Dusty Springfield, alongside the classic soul of James Brown, Ocean Colour Scene's 'Hundred Mile High City', the Stone Roses' 'Fools Gold', plus the Castaways, Stretch and the theme from *Zorba the Greek*.

diamond heist story, which would twist and turn more than an East End eel in a bucket of jelly, demanded tough-looking characters from Irish gypsy, Orthodox Jewish, Afro-Caribbean, Chinese and white working-class communities, plus one or two Russians and Scots.

Jason Statham was, inevitably, one of the first names on the *Snatch* team-sheet. He'd play Turkish, a small-time promoter who muscles in on the lucrative business of illegal underground boxing, and becomes dangerously embroiled with 'The Mob' over the whereabouts of a stolen diamond. It's interesting to note that Jason's role in *Snatch* started small – perhaps Guy Ritchie was worried that he wouldn't cope in such star-studded company – but expanded during the filming process. By the time it reached post-production, Jason's Turkish was the film's narrator as well as one of its main protagonists.

Following *Lock Stock & Two Smoking Barrels*, and with international film backing from the outset, naturally there were greater expectations, and increased demands, to deliver business at the box office. It wouldn't be enough to succeed in the UK; this time Ritchie's film had to work worldwide. Jason hadn't felt this pressure but acknowledged that Guy Ritchie probably had: 'I'm sure there was more pressure but it was pretty much directed at Guy. He's the writer, he's the director, he's the centre of the movie.'

One way of alleviating the pressure would be to bring in several big names – established Hollywood film stars who would definitely attract punters and, importantly, appeal to American audiences and critics. Benicio del Toro, who played Frankie Four Fingers in *Snatch*, had appeared in Sean Penn's *Indian Runner* and Terry Gilliam's *Fear and Loathing in*

Las Vegas. Ex-Chicago-policeman-turned-actor Dennis Farina (Avi) had starred in *Miami Vice*, *Get Shorty* and *Saving Private Ryan*.

However, it would be the casting of the Irish gypsy character One-Punch Mickey O'Neil that would really put Guy Ritchie's second film on the map. Jason was asked about the famous actor early on. He replied, 'Yeah, Brad something right? Good-looking chap?'

Brad Pitt had seen *Lock Stock & Two Smoking Barrels* and had asked to be cast in Ritchie's next movie. SKA Producer Matthew Vaughn recalled their reaction: 'We were shocked at first, thinking "God, there's nothing in it for him." He normally gets $20 million a film but he agreed to a much smaller fee for *Snatch* ... and the same size trailer as everyone else!'

The timing of the production played a part in Pitt's decision. He'd just been shooting *Fight Club* (1998) with Edward Norton, so he was in peak condition to convincingly play Ritchie's physically tough, charismatic, pugilistic hard-man. But he still had to do some character research.

According to Jason, Brad was whisked off to a travellers' campsite to spend time with real gypsies and appreciate their lifestyle: 'The one we went to see was pretty straightforward like (*Jasons puts on an Irish accent*) "What the feck are you doing here?" We were wondering whether the car was gonna be left on bricks but fortunately it wasn't. You've got this stigma attached with these characters; sometimes they live up to it and sometimes they don't.'

Obviously, the presence of the Americans Pitt, Del Toro and Farina on set could only but inspire the rest of the cast – including diverse characters such as Mike *EastEnders* Reid,

Lennie James, Vinnie Jones, Rade Šerbedžija, Jason Ninh Cao and Stephen Graham – to raise their game. 'These are great actors,' remarked Jason at the time. 'Brad, Benicio, Dennis ... we knew that it was going to be great and they were going to enhance it completely. They were brilliant to have around ... I picked up a lot of stuff from them, but I don't think there's any great trick to acting.'

Dennis Farina later gave interesting insights into working on a film production with Guy Ritchie, stressing the import-ance of the Italian-style family bond or brotherhood that exists on the most harmonious film sets. But Dennis did have some personal difficulties to deal with first: 'I had a hard time understanding everyone ... I just got used to saying "Oh yeah sure" to everyone. Mechanically I had a hard time, too ... I kept getting into the wrong side of the car.'

Farina also found it unusual, almost old-fashioned, working as part of an all-male cast: 'We talked about things that guys talk about. I mean their football is not like our football, and I was asking Vinnie (Jones) to explain cricket to me and he asked me to explain American football to him ... it was what guys do when guys get together.'

Guy Ritchie has also spoken about his philosophy behind running a film production: 'It's not only about getting the right face and personality to play the part. It's about creating a family. That's why casting takes so long – the actors them-selves have to be very real and very strong and they also have to gel off-screen.'

Jason confirmed the feel-good family factor that exists behind the scenes on Ritchie's films: 'Working on one of Guy's films is the best fun you can have. He likes to have the same people around him: actors, cameramen, technicians ...

Celebrating on the red carpet with the cast and director of *Lock Stock…* at the US premiere in February 1999.

Jason enjoys a tender moment with his then girlfriend Kelly Brook in July 1999.

Jason as Turkish in *Snatch*, Guy Ritchie's 'gangster comedy of errors'.

Jason shows that diving and martial arts training
pays off in cult classic *The Transporter*

On the red carpet with Seth Green at the world premiere of *The Italian Job*.

Opposite: Jason and Mark Wahlberg on the set of the remake of the classic 1969 British crime caper *The Italian Job*.

Above: Following their move to Hollywood, Kelly remains at Jason's side at

Back in the multi-storey car park preparing for another mission, Jason's Frank Martin makes a spectacular return in *Transporter 2*.

the same sound technicians, lighting guys, the same director of photography. We're still just messing around, playing chess in between takes, playing practical jokes ... it's exactly the same.

This style of directing really paid off and added to the authenticity of the scenes. 'On *Snatch* we would be having such a laugh that sometimes we would forget we were supposed to be making a film. It's a great ensemble piece where there aren't any real leads. Except for the dog – he's the star. He was just uncontrollable – attacking everything, especially leather, which, unfortunately, featured highly in our wardrobe.'

The upbeat mood extended to comedy fines for simply 'being flash', being late or not turning off mobile phones on location – 'I got fined fifty quid because my mobile went off, even though I wasn't working at the time' – and there would be no shortage of practical jokes. When producer Matthew Vaughn turned up with a new Porsche, Jason and his henchmen filled the boot with rusty horseshoes. After spending time driving his expensive, struggling, straining new car around London, Vaughn apparently took it back to the garage for a check-up; when the mechanic opened the boot he realised what had happened.

The competitive friendship – some branded it a fraternal relationship – between Jason Statham and Guy Ritchie also continued to develop during *Snatch*. Both were adept at martial arts, with Ritchie being a judo black belt. More fiercely, Jason and Guy seemed to be locked in a lifelong battle for supremacy at chess. In press interviews, both continually claimed to be superior to their opponent. During *Snatch*, Ritchie remarked: 'After a long day's shooting I want to be able to have a pint with the lads and cash in on the money Statham owes me from our daily game of chess.' But, years later, Jason was still joking that Guy owed *him* 'loads of money for losing so many games of chess'.

If Guy Ritchie could capture some of this off-screen fun, and use it to good effect in *Snatch*, then surely he'd have another winner on his hands. But *Lock Stock & Two Smoking Barrels* would be a hard act to follow. Whereas in his first film a group of friends were unwittingly caught up in the underworld of drugs, crime and violence, according to Ritchie, 'in *Snatch*, the players are the underworld, but it is London villainy with a comic twist'.

With its tag-line of 'Stealing bones and breaking stones', *Snatch* was never intended to be a sequel to *Lock Stock* ... It was described in the advance publicity as 'a rollicking ride through London's gangster world, its bustling diamond district and a rowdy gypsy camp ... As plans go haywire and tempers fray, dogs, diamonds, mobile homes, boxers and assorted weaponry get swept up into a chaotic free-for-all ...'

As Jason explained, 'We all wheel and deal but to different degrees. Everyone's plans collide and go haywire, with the madcap nature of it all getting bigger and bigger and this diamond still floating around London.'

As with his first film, *Snatch* began with Jason centre-stage, this time as the narrator Turkish, a boxing promoter intriguingly named after a plane crash. On screen, Jason looked a lot more stylish than he had done in *Lock Stock* ... , particularly when he was dressed as a country squire during the hare-coursing sequence. As usual, he delivered his lines as if he had written them himself, for example, 'Who took the jam out of your doughnut?'

While the black comedic, cockney underworld of gangster-infested London was once again the setting for Ritchie's film, it was grimly realistic in parts with elements of the plot based on true stories. For example, when the villainous ganglord Brick Top (played by Alan Ford) talked about feeding his victims to pigs, Ritchie's script may well have been referring back to a late-1960s murder in Hertfordshire and other unsolved cases involving sinister disappearances. But it would also have macabre echoes of the case of Canadian serial killer and farmer Robert Pickton, who was said to have fed murdered prostitutes to his pigs. As Brick Top memorably said, for pigs 'the sight of a chopped-up body is like curry to a pisshead'.

Musically, Guy Ritchie once again assembled a diverse mix of songs to accompany his action, including classic tracks such as The Stranglers' 'Golden Brown', The Specials' 'Ghost Town' and 10cc's 'Dreadlock Holiday'. Especially memorable was an extremely violent sequence featuring Vinnie Jones, in which the victim was trapped in an electric car window, cut to the sounds of 'Lucky Star' by Mrs Ritchie (a.k.a. Madonna).

When *Snatch* was released on 1 September 2000, the film struggled to charm or impress the critics in the same way that *Lock Stock & Two Smoking Barrels* had. Although the *Daily Express* described it as 'a barrel of fun, even better than *Lock Stock*', generally the reviews expressed confusion at the tangled web of a plot. Guy Ritchie's cinematic style – so strikingly free and original when *Lock Stock ...* came out – now seemed more predictable and, perhaps, familiarity and jealousy (over his private life with Madonna) bred contempt from certain elements of the media.

In response to the inevitable backlash against Ritchie,

Jason Statham was incredibly supportive and positive about *Snatch*: 'The thing about the UK is that we don't make that many great movies. When I see a movie I want to be entertained, and I think Guy involves a lot of drama, a lot of action, a lot of comedy, there's a great story being told . . . it's visually entertaining . . . all these things, when put together, make an overtly entertaining film.'

While Dennis Farina and Benicio del Toro definitely enhanced the proceedings in their very different, stylish ways, it was inevitably Brad Pitt who attracted most critical attention. Although he gives a typically charismatic, strong physical performance as One Punch Mickey O'Neil, his attempt at an Irish gypsy accent caused several film critics to sharpen their pens. *Empire* recommended subtitles, while *Total Film* branded his impression as reminiscent of Dick Van Dyke's cockney chimney sweep in *Mary Poppins*.

If *Snatch* didn't make the same splash as *Lock Stock & Two Smoking Barrels* had, it could still boast the biggest movie premiere of any 18-rated British film in history and, more importantly for its backers, it would generate $80 million in box office receipts. The presence of American stars, particularly Brad Pitt, had given *Snatch* greater audience clout internationally and, without doubt, propelled some of the lesser-known British cast members into the sights and contact books of big-league American film producers.

If *Lock Stock* . . . had launched Jason Statham to stardom in the UK, then without doubt – top of the bill, alongside Brad Pitt – *Snatch* transformed him into an international film star; he would soon find himself playing cards with Pitt and Vinnie Jones at their homes in Hollywood.

Within two years Jason had gone from street-hustler-

male-model to major British film star with immense potential. Very soon he would be working with director John
Carpenter on *Ghosts of Mars* and with one of his martial arts
heroes, Jet Li, on *The One*. And, of course, he'd soon be in
production again with Guy Ritchie and Vinnie Jones on *Mean
Machine*. There was absolutely no chance of Jason forgetting
where he came from or who had helped him get to Hollywood:
'I pretty much will do any project that Guy's going to direct.
It doesn't really take much for me to consider working with
him. He's a terrific director and I love to be a part of anything
that he does. I love his films. As silly as that might sound,
he's the man, really; he gave me a career and I'll be forever
in debt to him.'

CHAPTER FOUR:

MR KELLY BROOK

It was one of the most celebrated and admired relationships of the late 20th/early 21st century. Alongside the celebrity pairings of David Beckham and Posh Spice, Catherine Zeta Jones and Michael Douglas, Tom Cruise and Katie Holmes, Guy Ritchie and Madonna, and Brad Pitt and Jennifer Aniston (followed by Brad Pitt and Angelina Jolie), the seemingly solid-as-a-rock partnership of glamour-model-turned-TV-personality Kelly Brook and street-hustler-turned-film-star Jason Statham presented a fascinating, less glitzy, more down-to-earth, thoroughly English public image.

But what really set them apart from the other glamorous couples who strutted down red carpets at international movie premieres and major awards ceremonies was the fact that their love affair had begun before either of them had become famous. From the outside, it looked like the perfect opposites-attract, working-class match. Brook: young, beautiful, curvaceous, stylish and unpretentious, with a smile that could light up London. Statham: older, rugged, no-nonsense, protective, serious, tough-looking man about town. Sarah Chalmers of the *Daily Mail* described their relationship as 'one of the strongest partnerships in the notoriously fickle world of showbusiness'.

The couple had first met back in 1997 when Jason, then in his twenties, was making a name for himself as a male model while coming to terms with the end of his international diving career. He recalled seeing the seventeen-year-old Kelly Ann Parsons while modelling on the Greek island resort of Santorini: 'I was just bowled over. I thought she was the most amazing girl I had ever seen. She had an instant effect on me.'

Their relationship developed from there. Despite the age difference, they were both from similar, solid working-class backgrounds. He was living in Sydenham, South London, whereas she was half-an-hour down the A2 in Rochester, Kent. While Jason's parents ran street auctions, Kelly's father was a scaffolder and her mother's profession has variously been described as a 'food technician' or, more poetically, 'working in a pie shop'. Kelly later recalled her early encounters with Jason: 'I knew him when I was seventeen and he was working down the markets, driving a little battered blue van.'

Some sources suggest they first started going out seriously after appearing together at a recording for Chris Evans' *TFI Friday* show for Channel Four in 1998, but they were firm friends long before then. In the early days, according to local sources, they shared a flat on Lawrie Park Road, SE26, not far from the National Sports Centre at Crystal Palace, where Jason had done his diving training. This area could definitely be described as the 'home turf' of their relationship; several years later, in 2004, they were both hospitalised after Kelly's Mini crashed near Sydenham Park.

Tabloid-reading males first became aware of Kelly Parsons in her disrobed role as a glamour model and forces pin-up. At 5 feet, 8 inches, and with (to adopt the choice language of a retro *Miss World* voice-over) 'gravity-challenging vital statistics of 32E-24–35', she looked unfashionably curvy in a modelling era dominated by the slim-line Kate Moss.

After a tacky start (bad pun intended) posing seductively for a local carpet firm's advertising campaign – slogan: 'the only way to get laid' – Kelly was rescued by *Daily Star* photographer Jeany Savage, who changed the model's name to Kelly Brook, gave her a classy make-over and turned her into a firm favourite of both the lad mags and the red tops. As Brook once remarked, for 'a lady of my shape . . . it was only ever going to be lingerie and swimwear'.

Initially she was right, securing modelling deals with companies such as Bravissimo, promoting 'Big Bras, Lingerie, Swimwear and Clothing for D-KK Cup Women'. But, more importantly, she was naturally beautiful with a brilliant smile and, as her popularity increased, she was in demand for diverse campaigns such as Foster's Lager, Walkers crisps, the Renault Mégane and Piz Buin suncream. She also appeared in the promo video for Pulp's 'Help the Aged'.

In the late 1990s, when her boyfriend Jason moved on from Kit Kat ads, modelling assignments and pop videos into the big-league business of British cinema with *Lock Stock & Two Smoking Barrels*, Kelly Brook was also being presented with new opportunities. Having tried her hand at studio presentation on youth-orientated channels such as MTV and the lad-mag equivalent of television, Granada's *Men & Motors*, in January 1999 she beat a variety of contenders (including Gail Porter and the model Caprice) to replace Denise van Outen on Channel Four's *The Big Breakfast*.

She had doubts about taking the job, as she'd tell *The Observer*'s Polly Vernon in 2004. 'I remember having the conversation with my mum. "Are you sure? Are you sure you want to do this? Are you ready? Ooh God Kelly, it's a bit of a big thing for you to do this early on." But I thought, "Oh why not, what have I got to lose? If it doesn't work out I'm young enough, I'm resilient, I can bounce back ... " It was an opportunity that landed in my lap, it wasn't something I'd always wanted. I didn't really care. Perhaps that's why it wasn't the success it should have been. Perhaps I should have cared more.'

Kelly Brook had just turned nineteen when she joined the show. The special chemistry between Johnny Vaughan and Van Outen had helped the live morning programme achieve its best ratings since original host Chris Evans quit in 1994. With Kelly sitting in the hot seat alongside Vaughan, *The Big Breakfast* remained watchable, but not always for the right reasons. Live television is a difficult skill to master, even for veteran broadcasters, and it soon became painfully clear that the programme-makers had chosen Brook primarily because of her looks and her potential appeal to their target audience.

An internal memo leaked from the production company Planet 24, in the summer of 1999, claimed she couldn't pronounce long words such as 'satirical' and 'intrepid'. They urged scriptwriters to keep her lines simple and stressed that 'alliteration and obscure words' should be 'kept to a minimum'. Fuelled by newspaper criticisms of her struggle to cope with live television, and the unavoidable comparisons with the older and more experienced Denise van Outen –

who had seemed more comfortable on screen – Brook was considered by parts of the media to be less intelligent than her predecessor. Depending on which version of the story you choose to believe, she either quit or was dropped from *The Big Breakfast* while on holiday with Jason in the Canary Islands: 'Some pretty cruel stuff was said,' she admitted, 'but I was super-in-love. *The Big Breakfast* was so secondary. I was like, "Who cares? I can't wait for this show to finish" ... so I could go home and kiss him.'

This negative experience would have destroyed many teenagers, but instead Kelly Brook and Jason Statham moved to Los Angeles in 2000 to escape growing British media attention and restart their life together in Hollywood. While Jason's career had continued to develop since *Lock Stock & Two Smoking Barrels* and *Snatch*, Kelly had found it difficult to escape from the shadows of her *Big Breakfast* experience. An attempt by her former employers, Planet 24, to interview her for a documentary celebrating the Channel Four early morning show was met with a brilliantly blunt fax: 'Kelly gone to Hollywood'.

But arriving in Hollywood, twenty years old, initially living with Jason in his old friend Vinnie Jones' palatial LA home, Kelly was hardly starting from scratch. Through Jason and his growing legion of contacts in Tinseltown, she found herself rubbing shoulders with stars such as Brad Pitt (Statham's co-star in *Snatch*) and his new wife Jennifer Aniston, and Guy Ritchie and *his* then-wife Madonna. 'They're just friends to us,' Kelly said. 'They've never been anything less than warm and hospitable to me.'

Together, Jason and Kelly bought a two-bedroom Mexican-style villa in Beverly Hills and, by Statham's account, tried to avoid the celebrity high life. Years later, Kelly would credit Jason with teaching her to lead a healthy lifestyle to help develop her career: 'Jason was so health-conscious and so clean in what he ate. He gave me loads of books, like *Fit for Life* [by Ranulph Fiennes]. Not only did my body change, but my energy levels were amazing. Since then, I've always been aware.'

Inevitably, the move to Los Angeles gave her the confidence to move on and do something else; to escape the British tabloid press image of her simply as a glamour model and failed TV presenter. As she told *The Observer*: 'It was a clean slate . . . My accent and my character . . . they responded to it better. Here, I was sort of bubbly TV presenter, ex-glamour model . . . there, I was English and, hmmm, sweet.'

If you read back through the interviews and articles about Kelly Brook's life with Jason, what shines through is the sense that she's liked by both men and women. For example, she topped *FHM*'s '100 Sexiest Women in the World' poll but also was voted 'Best British Female Body' in a *Grazia* magazine poll of 500 women. She comes across as warm and funny, unpretentious and self-deprecating, less self-confident and clever than Catherine Zeta-Jones, and physically more like a brunette British Marilyn Monroe with a giggling Barbara Windsor element thrown in. The *Daily Mail* once observed that 'the real secret of her success is her sincere nature coupled with humility which comes from public failure'.

Indeed, rather than causing her to self-destruct, Kelly's very public failure to make the grade on *The Big Breakfast* had only made her more determined. 'It gave me the motivation to prove myself,' she said. She could have chosen to stay out of the spotlight for a year or two, but clearly was not one to avoid useful publicity. Within months she was back, starring in Triumph's Flaunt campaign, modelling underwear for curvaceous women. She also took a stage role, pole-dancing in the play *Eye Contact* at the Riverside Studios in Hammersmith, west London.

More strikingly – while Jason was away on location in New Mexico filming John Carpenter's *Ghosts of Mars* with the rapper Ice Cube – Brook stepped out, Liz Hurley-style, with Vinnie Jones and Brad Pitt at the premiere of *Snatch* in August 2000. She wore a pink see-through Julien MacDonald dress with a highly visible matching pair of sequinned knickers. The *Daily Mail* described the outlandish costume as 'the skimpiest dress in history'. She was making a statement, attracting the attention of the Warner Brothers producers, and announcing to the world that she still had the confidence and sex appeal to turn heads.

Speaking of the premiere, Jason later told the *Birmingham Post*, 'I was truly gutted that I couldn't go. It would have been such a big deal, even better than the one for *Lock Stock & Two Smoking Barrels* ... but I had filming commitments and I couldn't let people down.' As for Kelly? 'I thought she looked fantastic. She told me she had got a lovely outfit and I like her wearing sexy things. That was another reason why I wish I had been there.' But he did reveal that Kelly would be joining him soon: 'I can't wait. I haven't seen her for a while and anything more than two, three weeks without her drives me mad. Anything more than a couple of days does . . . It won't happen again. Hopefully we can work in the same place from now on.'

To cite the late, great philosopher and thinker John Lennon, life is what happens to you while you're busy making other plans. Professionally, Jason's film career was reaching extraordinary heights. Between 2000 and 2004, he would be acclaimed as the first great action hero of the new millennium for his role as Frank Martin in *The Transporter* and – once he had played Handsome Rob in the remake of *The Italian Job* – Hollywood first began to see him as the main contender to replace the old guard of leading men such as Bruce Willis, Arnold Schwarzenegger, Sylvester Stallone, Mel Gibson, and even Clint Eastwood.

With his martial arts background, some critics made positive comparisons between Jason and the great Chuck Norris, who'd battled Bruce Lee in *The Way of the Dragon* (1972). Audiences, male and female, seemed to believe in him, and suddenly Statham was proving to be a more versatile actor than anyone in Britain or the USA had expected or predicted. His accelerating career – which would see him take on a variety of challenging roles over the next few years – meant that it was probably inevitable that his personal life would have to take a back seat.

Meanwhile, Kelly Brook was also making a small name for herself in British and American cinema. In 2000 she appeared in the well-made London drugs- and club-scene thriller *Sorted* (directed and written by Alex Jovy) alongside Tim Curry, Matthew Rhys and Jason Donovan. She also won a role in the *Superman* spin-off *Smallville* as Lex Luthor's lover Victoria Hardwick and there were high hopes of her starring in a *Bewitched*-style US TV show titled *The (Mis)Adventures of Fiona Plum*. Other minor film roles followed, including Marisa Tavares in the Canadian film *Ripper: Letter from Hell* and in the sci-fi thriller *Absolon* with Christopher Lambert (2003). That same year she had a very brief but beautiful, closing-scenes cameo playing Lyle's girlfriend in *The Italian Job* remake (which also starred Jason).

Despite her modelling career and her *Big Breakfast* experience, with Jason's backing Kelly Brook had transformed her career in a remarkably short time. But it was hardly comparable with Catherine Zeta-Jones' journey from *The Darling Buds of May* to Hollywood, to Michael Douglas and eventually an Oscar for her role in *Chicago*. Brook's early film CV, did not suggest that there were Academy Awards on the horizon. Nevertheless, an indication that she could indeed act in a leading role came in Sue Heel's *School for Seduction* (2004). She played the glamorous Italian teacher Sophia Rosselini, who arrives in the North East of England to educate working-class women (played by Dervla Kirwan, Margi Clarke and Emily Woof) in the arts of seduction and female empowerment. *Movie Gazette* hailed it as 'a welcome addition to the multi-narrative ensemble comedy at which British cinema seems to excel', while the BBC described it as 'the rarest of British movies; one aimed primarily at women'. Its target audience was arguably the complete opposite of Guy Ritchie's.

In January 2004, on a return visit to their old haunts near Sydenham Park in south-east London, Kelly and Jason were involved in a car accident and were both treated for minor injuries at Lewisham University Hospital. With hindsight, this could be seen as the beginning of a less happy period for the celebrity couple.

At around this time, Jason had answered a journalist's question about the prospect of his starring with Kelly in a romantic film: 'It would feel really weird. I know Tom Cruise and Nicole Kidman did it, but as far as I'm concerned we'll keep it for our private life.'

The next, most obvious stage in the Statham-Brook relationship would have been to settle down in Beverly Hills and have California-born kids, or adopt children from some godforsaken part of Africa. But with Jason's action-hero star rising and Kelly being fought over by film production companies and advertising brands, perhaps something, eventually, had to give. They'd been officially together for almost seven years when Kelly Brook started work on the desert-island thriller *Survival Island* (a.k.a. *Three*).

As a production, it would have a seismic impact on Kelly's personal life if not her professional career, and likewise would greatly affect Jason as well. Shot in Greece and bizarrely similar to *Swept Away*, which Guy Ritchie had unsuccessfully remade with Madonna as recently as 2002, the plot focused on a torrid love triangle between Brook's white-bikini-clad character Jennifer and her co-stars Billy Zane and Juan Pablo Di Pace. Robert Hancock of *The Independent* slated it as 'an unholy amalgam of *Lord of the Flies*, *The Blue Lagoon* and *The Admirable Crichton* ... at odd moments it rises to risibility, but mostly it is just dull'. Jonathan Trout, writing for *BBC Movies*, described it as 'ham-fisted, bone-headed, leaden-footed and breast-obsessed' and stated that '*Three* encompasses a whole physiology of awfulness'. Ideally, it would have received limited publicity and disappeared to DVD.

However, the media fascination with *Survival Island/Three* went into overdrive in the summer of 2004 when Kelly was photographed arm-in-arm with her co-star Billy Zane in St. Tropez. Zane had starred in major Hollywood movies such as *Dead Calm*, *Memphis Belle*, *The Phantom* and, most famously, *Titanic*, playing the rich, bullying Cal Hockley, who was dumped by Kate Winslet's Rose in favour of the poor-but-beautiful Jack (Leonardo DiCaprio).

Although Chinese whispers of an affair between Brook and

Zane were initially denied by Kelly, Jason and Billy's publicist, rumours continued to spread and press reports suggested that, in August 2004, Statham had ordered Brook back to Los Angeles for 'crisis talks'.

Having initially ridiculed the stories by telling journalists, 'You've got it wrong ... Kelly's never been to St. Tropez in her life', Jason must have felt betrayed and emotionally humiliated by what followed.

Kelly Brook now had to make the most difficult decision of her life; to stay with Jason, her first real boyfriend, or to end their previously rock-solid relationship and jump ship. Helpfully, the *Sunday Mirror* ran 'a fact file on both hunks to help Kelly make up her mind'. Billed as 'the Battle of the Baldies', it pointed out that Statham was 'on the up ... he's set for big things', whereas Zane was 'on the slide ... a fading star but has oodles of celeb pals and multi-million-pound producing deals ... definitely not short of a bob or two'.

By November 2004, when Kelly Brook was interviewed by *The Times*, she still seemed to be struggling with her decision to leave Jason. At one point she said, 'I'd like to think we could work things out ... but we'll see ... how it looks is kind of how it is really. It's confusing for all concerned.' Then, a week later, she told the *Observer* it was over with Jason and that 'I'm in love and enjoying a new relationship ... I'm just in love and it's with somebody else. And have been for a while. It's not new. It's just that everyone seems to think it's new and ... scandalous.'

In personal terms, it must have been an extremely traumatic time for Jason. Not only had he lost his girlfriend of seven years, but the separation also distanced him from Kelly Brook's family, who had treated him like their own son.

Did the break-up affect Jason's film work? It must have had some impact. Had, in the end, his obsession with his career – his competitive focus on what he wanted to achieve professionally – cost him the love of his life? Perhaps, afterwards, he ploughed his understandable anger and negative energy into the subsequent, more emotionally complex roles he was offered in films such as *London*, *Revolver* and *The Bank Job*.

For example, in New York, doing promotional interviews for Guy Ritchie's *Revolver*, which came out in 2005, Jason was asked if the film had enlightened him in any way. He responded: 'I think it's sort of about awareness, you know? If you're being a bit of an idiot, or being a bit too selfish, if you're aware of that, you're on a good side. I know a lot of people have problems, whether it be with gambling, drinking, drugs, women, infidelity ... whatever their problem is ... horses ... everyone's got a weakness ... And if you can understand that you have that vulnerability within you, and understand where that comes from, then you can only become a better person from that.'

Consider, also, the too-close-to-home role he would later take in *The Bank Job* (2008), playing Terry Leather, the used-car-dealer-turned-reluctant-bank-robber caught up in a messy love triangle. It was arguably the first drama since *Lock Stock & Two Smoking Barrels* that allowed Jason to reveal his natural acting talents without props, stunts and explosions, and it enabled him to convincingly display the emotions of a man in crisis. As *Bank Job* producer Charles Roven commented, 'The part of Terry really shows Jason's great range as an actor. It allows him to do it all, from being the tough guy to struggling with romantic conflict.'

In contrast, after her difficult summer of 2004, Kelly Brook was having fun with Billy Zane. As she told the *Observer*: 'I'm enjoying my new love, seeing the world with him ... I love working, but at the moment, I'm really enjoying living. I feel like I've let go of a lot of responsibilities and a lot of ties. I was free before but I feel freer now.' On the down side, Brook and Zane both tried – but failed – to have her on-screen sex scenes edited out of *Survival Island/Three*.

For several years it looked as if Billy Zane, instead of Jason Statham, would be the true love of Kelly Brook's life. Brook and Zane got engaged in 2007, bought a house in Kent, and were planning to get married in the summer of 2008.

During November 2007 – the period in which Kelly worked as one of the celebrity contestants on BBC1's *Strictly Come Dancing* – her father, Ken, died of cancer. Kelly bravely tried to complete the series but eventually withdrew from the competition. Instead of entering into marriage, she would terminate her engagement to Billy Zane in August 2008. The *Sun* reported the break-up with the headline: 'A Pain Called Zane Is Firmly Out Of The Frame'.

By and large, the lives of Jason Statham and Kelly Brook have developed in very different ways since they parted company. With few exceptions along the way, Jason's action-hero status and box-office potential has been enhanced by each new on-screen performance, from *Crank* through to *The Expendables*.

Aside from acting appearances in TV's *Hotel Babylon*, *Marple* and *Moving Wallpaper*, presenting *Celebrity Love Island* and judging *Dirty Dancing: The Time of Your Life* and, very briefly, *Britain's Got Talent*, Kelly Brook made high-profile stage appearances in Neil LaBute's *Fat Pig* and as Celia in *The Calendar Girls*, both in London's West End. She also used her modelling status to secure several big-money-earning advertising campaigns, including Ultimo, Reebok and a million-pound deal for Lynx body spray.

In terms of cinema roles, however, Brook's decisions have been less astute than Jason's. Returning to her glamour-model roots, often dressed in her bikini or even less, she was written off as a 'soft-core titan' by one Hollywood critic, who suggested her 2010 B-movie horror thriller *Piranha 3D* should be re-titled Piranha 3DDD: 'a rip-off of *Jaws* ... a relentless onslaught of T&E – tits and entrails'. *Total Film* was more positive but nevertheless stated the *Carry On* obvious: 'Kelly Brook has had her knockers but no one can accuse her of not making the most of her assets' before claiming that the film was 'an entertaining rehash of the old Roger Corman classic'.

To her immense credit, Kelly has always seemed self-deprecating and immune from all the criticism directed her way. Of nudity she once said, 'I'm so used to it by now that I'm more terrified of putting my clothes on! I haven't got any huge body hang-ups. I've got to the age where I've accepted all flaws. I know I'm never going to be perfect.'

More recently – in this publicity-hungry, celebrity-obsessed age, in terms of what is laughably still called 'private life' – Kelly Brook was in a two-year relationship with the talented young English rugby player Danny Cipriani until June 2010. Jason, meanwhile, has been pictured – and linked – with assorted beautiful women over the past five years. Post-Kelly, there was a short 'follow-up fling' with the Aussie singer-turned-actress Sophie Monk. He's also had well-documented relationships with Alex Zosman and, from summer 2010, Victoria's Secret lingerie model and *Transformers* actress Rosie Huntington-Whiteley.

But there will always be immense tabloid interest in Jason Statham and Kelly Brook reuniting. It's as if, somehow, nostalgically and perhaps unrealistically, the world was a better place when they were together and in love. Hence the media excitement back in early March 2010, when they were pictured 'enjoying an intimate lunch date' (according to *Now Magazine*) at Malibu's Greek restaurant Taverna Tony. The magazine's anonymous source commented: 'They've known each other for a long time, so when they're in the same city they'll catch up. Jason's got a new girlfriend and Kelly's happy with Danny Cipriani so there's little chance of them getting back together.'

Inevitably, the *News of the World* went with the headline: 'Kelly Lets Ex Love Jason Nibble Her Melon', before adding that 'they are good pals despite a painful split six years ago and meet whenever they are in the same part of the world'.

Heat magazine soon went into more detail, helpfully explaining that, barely one month after splitting from Danny Cipriani, Kelly was now terrified of being single and wanted to get back into a relationship as soon as possible. They reported that Kelly had phoned Jason to ask him to find her a guy in Los Angeles, quoting another anonymous source as saying, 'she's contacted Jason to see if he has any single pals she could line up for dates in Los Angeles. She actually really trusts his judgement.'

The same source, also quoted in London's *Evening Standard*, added, 'she doesn't have to look far – men fall over themselves to date her . . . But Kelly is phobic about being single. She feels like her brand is a million times stronger when she has a boyfriend in her life. She worries about her career and knows she makes column inches with her relationships and figure.'

The *Sun* claimed that 'TV Kelly "Rings Up Jason Every

Day"'. Their source added: 'He's a nice guy and still has a soft spot for her. Kelly is desperate to land more work in Hollywood and wanted his advice.' It is hard to find out what these reports are based on but given this level of interest and speculation about their romantic futures, it's no wonder that the paparazzi were desperately seeking the big-money shot of Jason and Kelly together at the premiere of *The Expendables*. They were disappointed.

Whatever the facts, whatever the fiction, despite the bitter end of their relationship in 2004, there's obviously still a closeness between Jason and Kelly that perhaps stems from their similar backgrounds, their youthful love affair and their extraordinary shared journeys from the London suburbs to the hills of Hollywood. And there's also a sense of regret, if only in interviews with Kelly, that they had been unable to avoid the obvious pitfalls of successful celebrity lives. As she said in 2007, 'Jason's career was also blossoming and it was difficult for us to see as much of each other as we would have liked. Like so many other couples it soon became clear that our relationship was faltering at the hands of the Hollywood lifestyle.'

Even with their hectic international jet-set lives and transatlantic professional schedules, it seems that Jason Statham and Kelly Brook have been able to remain firm friends. As Kelly once told Chrissy Iley of the *Sunday Times*, 'A big chunk of my life has been with Jason. We still speak from time to time to check in with each other. Ultimately we love each other and there is no animosity between us whatsoever.'

Whatever happens to Jason and Kelly in the future, he'll always have a leading role in her story and she'll always play a significant part in his.

CHAPTER FIVE:

TRANSPORTED TO HOLLYWOOD

Jason Statham had ended the 20th century as a rookie actor in Guy Ritchie's first feature – one of four loveable rogues leading the ensemble cast in a highly original British gangster film. Having grabbed this initial chance, the next stage in his meteoric rise to stardom had been playing alongside Brad Pitt in *Snatch* (released September 2000). Within eighteen months he'd been transformed from international-diver-stroke-market-trader-stroke-male-model into one of the UK's most likeable and interesting character actors.

Hardly an obvious-looking leading man, with his shaven head and often-scowling 'working-class' face, many viewers and reviewers probably felt that he'd already reached his zenith as a film actor. Surely, without dramatic experience and with only two Guy Ritchie film roles under his belt, Jason's thespian star couldn't rise much higher. Perhaps, moving to Hollywood in 2000 with his then-girlfriend Kelly

Brook, the former high diver was already out of his depth?

Jason clearly had different goals. He seemed dismayed by the inevitable backlash against Guy Ritchie and *Snatch*, and had also been annoyed by the British media's criticisms of Kelly in *The Big Breakfast*. Interviewed by *IGN* in early January 2001, he was asked why he'd quit the London he knew and loved, and why he'd moved away from his family and friends for an uncertain future battling for film roles in Los Angeles. Did he really believe there were better opportunities for him in Hollywood? 'I think so,' he had responded, 'because it has more great film-makers per square inch than anywhere in the world, but I don't want to turn my back on anything in Europe, because you know I started there. The thing about the UK is that we don't make that many great movies. The very few we do make we might say "Oh you should leave it alone, try not to mess it up". You know . . . it's just people's negativity back at home; it's just a general attitude amongst the nation.'

He was arguably right about the state of British cinema at the close of the 20th century. The only real major British films of 1999 were *Human Traffic*, *Notting Hill* and the latest James Bond adventure, *The World is Not Enough*, but 2000 would look more positive – with hindsight, at least. Apart from *Snatch*, there would be *The Beach*, *Gladiator*, *Calendar Girls*, Ken Loach's *Bread and Roses*, and Stephen Daldry's *Billy Elliot*.

In his favour, Jason now had strong connections in Hollywood. Even though Guy Ritchie's talents as a director would soon become more focused on his new wife Madonna's film aspirations – notably the disappointing *Swept Away* (2002), branded 'soggy and superfluous' by the *New York Times* – Ritchie still had the power, talent, confidence and drive to make things happen in the film world.

There was his underrated BMW-backed short film *The Hire: Star* (2001) – based on the interesting premise of a chauffeur (Clive Owen) transporting a rock star (Madonna) – followed by his involvement as Executive Producer on *Mean Machine*, a smart attempt to re-make Robert Aldrich's classic 1974 prison movie *The Longest Yard* (starring Burt Reynolds) in the style of a British *Porridge*-meets-*Lock Stock* comedy. Various members of the *Lock Stock & Two Smoking Barrels* cast also climbed on board the bandwagon alongside Ritchie, and notable among them were the former Wimbledon and Leeds footballer Vinnie Jones, Vas Blackwood, Jason Flemyng and – playing the psychotic Scottish goalkeeper – Jason Statham.

Ahead of filming *Mean Machine*, Jason told an American reporter: 'You know it's about an American footballer who goes to prison and rounds up the cons to play the prison guards. We're doing an English remake of that with soccer ... It's set in an English prison. I'm working with Vinnie Jones, he's a friend of mine who I've worked with on two movies now, and Matthew Vaughn is the producer who produced *Snatch* and *Lock Stock* ... It's like a family getting back together and doing a little English movie, and soccer is a big thing back home. We'll see how well it does, but I can guarantee you we'll have some fun making it.'

Although many high-brow critics at the time felt that *Mean Machine*'s first-time director Barry Skolnick shouldn't have touched Aldrich's original with a bargepole, the remake cleverly offered a violent but funny reworking of Tracy Keenan Wynn's screenplay and starred Vinnie Jones in the role of Mad Danny Meehan. As a professional footballer, Jones' presence guaranteed the physical authenticity now expected from every production involving Ritchie, Vaughn and SKA:

'The tackles are pretty damn good,' declared Vinnie, 'there is no moody fake stuff in it. What you see is proper football.'

The intention behind this comedic film was primarily to combine Vinnie Jones' footballing talents with his rising reputation as a British movie hard-man. But, even in the company of Jones and David Hemmings' addicted-to-gambling prison governor, Jason Statham performance is one of *Mean Machine*'s real strengths. Even American critics, who seemed baffled by the relocation of Aldrich's film from the American football field to the British 'soccer' pitch, noted Jason's unsettling screen presence and the deep menace in his eyes and voice. Forever-in-solitary-confinement Monk, as one of his scared fellow inmates observed, was the man who ate Hannibal the Cannibal, the man who had killed twenty-three people with his bare hands, before taking up peaceful karate.

Nevertheless, Jason's role in *Mean Machine* further cemented his close friendship with fellow South Londoner and action man Vinnie Jones. Indeed, when Jason and Kelly Brook first moved to Los Angeles, they had stayed with Vinnie in his Hollywood home.

Jason's friend Guy Ritchie had failed to build on his early successes in Hollywood in the first half of the 2000s – marriage to Madonna, her career and fatherhood restricted his directing and writing output until 2005's *Revolver* – Jason kept a sharper focus on his incipient film stardom. Whatever the reasoning behind his relocation to the USA, he clearly believed his future would be better there than in the UK. Putting aside some of the criticisms of Guy Ritchie's films, Jason's personal performances in both *Lock Stock & Two Smoking Barrels* and *Snatch*, closely followed by *Mean Machine*, had definitely put him on the Hollywood radar. Back in the

UK, critics had expected him to become typecast as a gangland villain or a cameo-role cockney in B-movies. Maybe, they
believed, he would eventually end up in *EastEnders*. Indeed,
his physical presence, his shaven head and his gruff *'Leave it
out'*-style London accent seemed perfectly suited to Albert
Square. Although Jason had hinted at some basic, comedic
karate moves in *Mean Machine*, no one at this stage in his
new career seemed aware that he had any real special talents
to offer the action movie genre.

True, American producers had already started knocking on
his door, but the locations and settings couldn't have been
further removed from his home turf of South London. In
Robert Adetuyi's New York rap movie *Turn It Up*, Jason
appeared as the perfectly evil British drugs baron, Mr B,
exploiting two young, promising musicians, played by Pras
Michel from The Fugees and controversial rapper Ja Rule.

Billed in advance as hip hop's answer to Prince's *Purple Rain*,
the film received a lukewarm reception from critics and
bombed at the box office, recouping only one third of its estimated nine-million-dollar costs. The *New York Times* praised
Turn It Up for capturing 'the urgency, impatience and frus-
trations of impoverished musicians' but complained that it
deteriorated into another 'gory shoot-'em-up gangsta movie'.

Importantly for Jason's future career, his performances
for Guy Ritchie in *Lock Stock*, *Snatch* and *Mean Machine*, plus
his villainous screen presence in *Turn It Up*, brought him to
the attention of the veteran maverick writer/director/
composer John Carpenter (who was famous for fantasy/
horror successes such as *Halloween*, *Escape from New York*
and *Escape from LA*). Carpenter had already begun casting his
latest action-meets-sci-fi-meets-horror movie, *Ghosts of Mars*.

Following his gut instinct for raw talent, Carpenter had initially decided that Jason would be perfect to play his futuristic central character, James Desolation Williams, a dangerous criminal on the run from Martian police. As a result, Jason is believed to have turned down a leading role in Neil Marshall's cult British werewolf horror film, *Dog Soldiers* (2002). Unfortunately, Carpenter's confidence in Jason was not shared by his producers and financiers, who demanded a more established star – a bigger box-office name – to play the part of Desolation opposite Natasha Henstridge's Lieutenant Melanie Ballard. Jason would later confirm this: 'John Carpenter saw me in *Lock Stock & Two Smoking Barrels* and set up a meeting. He wanted me to play the prisoner the cops have to transport in *Ghosts of Mars*, but the studio insisted he cast a higher-profile actor.'

Rather than dumping Jason, Carpenter offered him the role of Henstridge's cop sidekick Sgt Jericho Butler. Meanwhile, the producers' choice of 'higher-profile actor' turned out to be Ice Cube, the ex-NWA rapper, songwriter and star of *Boyz n the Hood* (1991), who sadly failed to deliver the level of commercial success required. Although Jason did not secure the main part as he had hoped, he clearly enjoyed the whole strange sci-fi filming experience: 'It's great,' he said on location in Mexico, 'there are lots of action scenes and running around with guns. The gypsum mine, which is supposed to be the surface of Mars, was bright white so they have to dye it red with thousands of gallons of food colouring.'

How had working with Carpenter compared with working on a Guy Ritchie film? 'It's a bit more serious but it's still fun,' claimed Jason. 'John's got a great sense of humour and I've been a fan of his films for years.' For all its faults, *Ghosts*

Of Mars also presented him with a rare early romantic role by offering him his first screen kiss, with Natasha Henstridge.

For various complex and interconnected reasons, Jason's next film role would prove to be his most significant stepping stone since his debut in *Lock Stock & Two Smoking Barrels*. There had been little need for him to utilise his sporting fitness and powerful physique in the early movies, and few casting agents or producers were aware that he had learnt various mixed martial arts as part of his training regime as an international diver, or that he'd long been a fan of martial arts movies, name-checking stars of the genre, such as Bruce Lee and Jackie Chan, in interviews. He had also developed a competitive but friendly rivalry with Guy Ritchie in the days when they had practised jiu-jitsu while working together.

An ancient Japanese martial art, jiu-jitsu – which translates as 'science of softness' or 'gentle art' – had been the primary unarmed combat method used by the Samurais to disable armed opponents; the emphasis was on self-defence, turning an attacker's own force against themselves, throwing them off-balance and attacking nerves and pressure points. Jason and Guy Ritchie both trained in the style of Helio Gracie's Brazilian jiu-jitsu, which derived from Kodokan judo and focused on grappling and ground-fighting.

When Jason was offered a leading role alongside the cult Chinese martial artist, actor and film producer Jet Li, he literally jumped at the opportunity. He had been a fan of Jet's 1994 film *Fist of Legend* and Jet had also starred in the classic *Shaolin Temple* (1982), the *Once Upon a Time in China* film series and the huge commercial hit *Lethal Weapon 4* (1998). This would be the beginning of a great friendship between Jason and Jet; the start of an onscreen working relationship that would last for more than a decade, incorporating *War* in 2007 and *The Expendables* in 2010. 'I was a bit in awe of him,' Jason later recalled of their first meeting.

An unusual mix of martial arts and science fiction, in some respects the narrative of *The One* (2001) wasn't too far removed from John Carpenter's *Ghosts of Mars*. Playing 'multiverse' agent, Evan Funsch, Jason patrolled space, battling trouble-makers from different universes. Top of his most-wanted list was the power-crazed criminal Yu-Law, played by Jet Li, who was determined to hunt down and kill variations of himself in parallel universes. Yu-Law's aim was to destroy his counterpart on Earth, Los Angeles-based agent Gabriel Law, to steal his life force and become a god.

It was essentially a good-versus-evil story starring Jet Li in both the 'good' and 'bad' central character roles. 'Only one will survive,' went the marketing tag-line. 'In order to save the universe, he will have to face the fiercest enemy he has ever faced . . . himself'.

Explaining his role in the film, Jason said: 'I'm more of a soldier that they've brought in from a universe that's pretty chaotic. We come from an establishment where they recruit only the best of the best to be a multiverse agent, so we're supposed to be capable of dealing with people like the Bad Jet, Yu-Law. Although he's probably the worst we've ever met by a long, long way.'

Jason also revealed that he had acquired the role of MVA (multiverse) agent Evan Funsch through his new manager, Ace Media's Steve Chasman, who also looked after Jet Li. 'Steve told me about the project and I met with Jim [Wong] and Glen [Morgan] before Christmas [2000] and expressed my interest. Time passed and eventually they gave me the role. I was really, *really* thrilled.'

The One was scripted and directed by the writers of *The X-Files*, *Millennium* and *Space: Above and Beyond*, Morgan and Wong. Mixing science fiction with martial arts, one critic suggested that it was a strange movie for Jet Li to make. 'It's a winning combination,' responded Jason, 'the stuff that he's physically capable of doing, the charm and charisma he's got, combined with all the special effects ... it's the only way forward. I think it's a fantastic combination to take both those great attributes and blend them in and make something that is appealing.'

In an interview on the official Jet Li website, Jason spoke warmly about his great good fortune to be working with the famous martial arts star: 'Well, Jet's a pain in the ass,' he joked, before adding, affectionately and respectfully, 'actually he's the best fun really. He's always messing around and cracking jokes and he's got a great sense of humour, which a lot of people fail to keep these days, especially big stars. You meet them and some of them are very serious ... I've met a few of them recently. But he's great. With all his talents, and I'm a big fan of martial arts and I know about his capabilities, so to be in the company of him is like a little dream come true. I've seen a lot of his movies and the next thing you know I'm doing scenes with him and it's great.'

Most film reviewers seemed to find the plot of *The One* much too confusing – particularly as Jet Li portrays seventeen different personalities in the film – while spotting parallels with Jean-Claude Van Damme's *Timecop* (1994). But few failed to register Jason's emergence as a potential action hero. *The One* had offered him his first opportunity to show off his martial arts skills even though – as he would explain in promotional interviews – time restrictions and other production issues meant some of his best scenes were either scrapped before filming or not included in the film's final edit: 'They've had to slice down what I was going to be doing,' Jason admitted with some regret, 'which is very unfortunate because I was looking forward to it. I did a fair amount of martial arts myself; I did kick-boxing and other stuff, but you know, not close to being in the same league as some of the present company. But I've got a bit more experience than the regular actor, and I've been involved in sport for years so I'm quite a physical guy. It's a shame that none of that stuff's going to be in. The most challenging thing,' he laughed, 'would be doing an American accent for the first time.'

Working alongside Jet Li inevitably alerted major US producers and directors to Jason Statham's previously hidden talents. In less than three years he had already journeyed from playing a dodgy London street salesman in *Lock Stock* . . . , to kick-boxing with his Hollywood co-star in *The One*. Better still, he was now keeping the very best company to further his career. With Guy Ritchie proclaiming his talents in London and Los Angeles, and manager Steve Chasman exploring fresh opportunities for his action hero, Jason realised he was entering new action man territory: 'Let's face it, it's a lucrative market,' he would note. 'Who else is there now? There's Jackie Chan and Jet Li, but they're Asian.'

Aside from his developing professional relationship with both Steve Chasman and Jet Li, *The One* also introduced Jason to the great Hong Kong fight choreographer and director Corey Yuen. In terms of his martial arts film pedigree, Yuen's track record was impressive. Not only had he worked on several of Jason's favourite Jet Li films, including 1993's *The Legend* (a.k.a. *Fong Sai Yuk*) but, as a young man, he had appeared alongside Jackie Chan as an uncredited kung fu fighter in Bruce Lee's *Fist of Fury* (1972).

Talented people don't always make good films, as the history of Hollywood too often testifies, but the combined powers of Jason Statham, Cory Yuen and Steve Chasman would soon be further strengthened by the arrival of a script called *The Transporter*, co-written by Robert Mark Kamen (of *Karate Kid* and *Lethal Weapon 3* fame) and the great French writer/director and creative *tour de force* Luc Besson. The writers' aim was to appeal to the younger generation of movie-goers; fans of the action-hero genre who had failed to identify with fifty- and sixty-something acting institutions such as Mickey Rourke, Harrison Ford, Bruce Willis, Steven Seagal and Jean-Claude Van Damme.

If anyone was destined to work with Luc Besson, then surely it was Jason Statham. Jason had spent his teenage years developing as a diver, while Besson's early life seems to have been spent underwater. Born in Paris, Besson's parents were scuba-diving instructors and he developed a great passion for the aquatic world. Initially he'd wanted to become a marine biologist but later turned into a highly original television and film director. 'I was never polluted by the world of cinema,' he once said. 'My expression is a reflection of the world I have seen, and in that world everyone was barefoot in bathing suits, following the order of the sea, the natural order of sunrise and sunset.'

Luc Besson's 1988 film *The Big Blue* would have an impact on Jason in various ways. Visually stunning, it starred Jean-Marc Barr as Jacques Mayol, a young man with the physical constitution of a dolphin, who could dive deeper than any human had previously thought possible. Although the film was about deep-sea free diving, in contrast to Jason's high-board pool diving, Jean-Marc Barr would become Jason's scuba-diving instructor for the stunts on the first *Transporter* film.

Luc Besson would return to underwater filming for his acclaimed documentary *Atlantis* (1991), but his international reputation rested on the box-offices successes of his stylish action films such as *Subway*, *La Femme Nikita*, *The Professional* and *The Fifth Element* (starring Bruce Willis, Besson's future wife Milla Jovovich and his good friend Gary Oldman). Another important factor in the development of Besson's working relationship with Jason was his growing interest in the martial arts. This was illustrated by Besson's involvement in films such as *Ong-Bak* (2003) – often credited with rejuvenating Hollywood's interest in kung fu – *District 13* (2004) and *Unleashed* (with Jet Li) in 2005.

As Simon Lewis later wrote in the *Daily Mail*, 'it was French producer Luc Besson who first realised that an actor who knew what a toe-hold was, with Statham's looks, voice and presence, might be worth putting into an action film.' Looking back, Jason concurred: 'When I was first given a start by Guy Ritchie, he was making black-comedy dramas, not so much action movies. And it was only Luc Besson who gave me a shot at expressing a few of my sort of hidden capabilities in *The Transporter*.'

Jason's hidden capabilities would be dramatically revealed in the role of Frank Martin, the no-questions-asked 'delivery man' with a mysterious past, a violent present and an uncertain future. Far removed from the rather more decent, world-

85

defending, girl-charming James Bond, Frank Martin would always act independently; he wasn't a secret agent with an altruistic agenda, he was a mercenary who transports packages and sometimes people. He would deal with the Devil if there was cash up-front but only if the contract honoured his three rules of engagement: no names, never change the deal and never look in the package.

According to Roger Ebert, in his review for the *Chicago Sun Times*: 'unlike Bond, Martin is amoral and works only for money; we gather he lost any shreds of patriotism while serving in the British Special Forces, and now hires out his skills to support a lifestyle that includes an oceanside villa on the French Riviera that would retail at $30million, minimum.'

Frank Martin was a fascinating central character – a man of few words with a mysterious, troubled past, who rarely shows emotion or allows himself to get too involved with the women he encounters. There was, perhaps, an unspoken sense that Frank has been damaged or scarred in former relationships. Although he's always physically attracted to the girls throughout *The Transporter* series – and often fails to resist them – you never feel that they learn anything deeper about him. When it comes to sex, he's red-blooded; in terms of romance, he's a closed book.

Guy Ritchie's *Lock Stock & Two Smoking Barrels* and *Snatch* had both opened with striking images of Jason Statham. *The Transporter* started the same way. Waiting for instructions in a grimly lit multi-storey car park, Jason was seated in the driving seat of a black BMW; hard-faced, black-suited. He listened to the 'Allegro' from Mozart's *Concert for Clarinet in A Major* and pulled on his black gloves like an undertaker approaching a funeral.

It was a classy opening that immediately begged the question, who is this fascinating character? There was an apocalyptic darkness, a deep sense of foreboding, about Frank Martin. We instinctively knew that he was not going to be a taxi driver, not even in the psychotic style of De Niro and Scorsese's Travis Bickle. But, in Hollywood screenwriting terms, we were left wondering if he was the protagonist or the antagonist? Was he a good guy who does bad things, or a bad guy who does terrible things?

We never learn much more about Frank Martin's backstory; only that he had been in the Special Forces. Early on, his *Transporter* co-star Shu Qi finds a box of photographs and memories that could have revealed more but, typically, these are destroyed along with Frank's expensive Riviera home in a mafia-led rocket attack moments later. As the transporter Frank never wants to know what is in the package and never wants anyone else to discover who he is or what he might have done in the past. One of Frank's strengths was his strange, quiet, aloofness; distant until pushed too far. But when the trouble starts, suddenly he is full-screen, ruthless and right in your face.

Jason's taciturn role was reminiscent, in some ways, of his hero Clint Eastwood in *The Outlaw Josey Wales*. But whereas Clint's character outdrew and gunned down his enemies, Jason's Frank Martin beat them with his bare hands, in an almost balletic display of cool, controlled, fearless martial artistry – even in the middle of a garage flowing with oil. The *New York Times* observed, 'rather than recklessly killing his assailants, Mr Statham demurely shoots them in the thigh or knocks them out, demonstrating a moral scrupulousness not much seen in American movies since Roy Rogers retired'.

Once, when asked about Frank's complicated and enigmatic and superficially anti-violent character, Jason replied:
'I think he'd always rather talk his way out of a situation. He
has this very firm moral code. What he does is not necessarily
on the right side of the law, but it is instinctively good. He's
a good judge of what is proper and deep-seated and respectful.
I think people also respect someone who can deal with very
intense situations that don't necessarily go as planned. He
can get out of those situations with minimal amounts of
damage.' But in his quest for an easy life, Frank eschews
personal relationships. 'The way he protects that is not to
get involved with people, to live a very lonely life. It's quite
different from most of our lives, and that may be why we
find a bit of interest in it. Generally, we're much more sociable
and less inclined to deal with situations.'

With Corey Yuen and Louis Leterrier co-directing, and Luc
Besson and Steve Chasman co-producing, Jason played Frank
Martin as a hardened loner; an emotionally controlled but
attractively flawed anti-hero; a Mad Max-style post-millennial
action man. It was a topical tale of people-trafficking, with
Frank operating outside the law to protect the innocent. By
offering a window into the lavish lifestyles of the villains on
show, it refused to pretend that crime does not pay.

Mainly shot in the south of France, *The Transporter* was a
stylishly European movie – as fashionably French as Besson's
early works – with unbelievable action sequences and impos-
sible-seeming fight scenes. Jason rose to the challenge brilliantly, performing all his own stunts including white-knuckle
car chases, superbly choreographed hand-to-hand martial arts
combat and scuba-diving scenes.

Although some had reservations about the plot and execution of *The Transporter*, many critics in the UK and USA praised Jason's personal performance, commenting on his 'wily street-tough charm' and proclaiming him as a new and handsome leading man in the action-hero genre. The *Independent* noted '*The Transporter* has made Jason Statham a major Hollywood alpha male'. The *Orlando Sentinel* stated '*The Transporter* crosses over into Bond far-fetchedness in its plot and stunts, but it's still a noisy, goofy, cartoonishly violent ride'. The *Guardian*'s cautious critic, meanwhile, appreciated the fact that it 'filled the void left by the absence of Bond films'.

Some, no doubt stunned by his rapid transformation from London wide-boy to Tinseltown star, damned the actor with faint praise. *Variety*'s understated review suggested that 'although the former diver handles himself well physically, it's not evident here what additional qualities Statham might possess that would cause him to prevail over any number of other candidates for action stardom'.

Having learned from Guy Ritchie the importance of authenticity and the need to be convincing on screen, Jason felt strongly that he needed to be seen proving himself as an action hero: 'I want to do everything on camera rather than revert to the luxuries of CGI [computer-generated imagery].' It was a statement of intent rather than a macho philosophy, and it certainly threw down the gauntlet to other action actors.

The days of the hugely successful action movies of the 1980s had long gone. Aside from the unstoppable James Bond series, there had been nothing quite like *The Transporter* since *Die Hard*, *Rambo*, *Raiders of the Lost Ark* or *The Terminator*, and their stars (Willis, Stallone, Ford, Schwarzenegger) had begun to look expendable; they certainly couldn't compete with Jason Statham when it came to performing realistic stunts. Their successors (Van Damme, Snipes, Seagal) headed for the straight-to-DVD market, and relative newcomers such as Vin Diesel and Dwayne 'The Rock' Johnson sometimes failed to have the impact that Hollywood studios had hoped for.

Often success is as much about timing as it is about talent. By 2001, when *The Transporter* went into production, there had been a lull in output from the James Bond production line. Pierce Brosnan's time as 007 was coming to an end and his last Bond film – *Die Another Day* (2002) – would be the twentieth in a forty-year series. Daniel Craig wouldn't slip into James' shiny shoes and tight trunks until 2006's *Casino Royale*. By then, Jason Statham's *The Transporter*, another Jason (Matt Damon's assassin Jason Bourne in *The Bourne Identity* and *The Bourne Supremacy*), and Tony Jaa in the kung fu footsteps of Jackie Chan and Jet Li, had upped the stakes in terms of box-office action movies. It is no coincidence that three of the most original action films of the 2000s – *The Transporter, Ong-Bak* and *Taken*, starring Liam Neeson – all greatly benefited from the production involvement of Luc Besson.

Made for the relatively small budget of $21million (*The Expendables*, in contrast, would cost more than $80million), *The Transporter* proved to be a resounding hit with action-film audiences worldwide, grossing $44million and confirming Jason's status as a major box-office attraction. No one knew it at the time, but this would be the launch of a three-film franchise that would almost dominate the genre throughout the decade, and one which, in 2003–2004, would lead to Jason appearing alongside major Hollywood names such as

Charlize Theron and Mark Wahlberg in the remake of *The Italian Job*, Tom Cruise and Jamie Foxx in *Collateral* and Kim Basinger in *Cellular*.

Often lazily referred to as 'the British Bruce Willis', Jason was now a bankable international star capable of earning serious money. It was estimated that he received $750,000 for his work on *The Transporter* and a further $450,000 for his role in *The Italian Job*.

Inevitably, given the box-office impact of the first film, *Transporter 2* was soon in production. Co-written again by Luc Besson and Robert Mark Kamen, with Besson and Steve Chasman producing, the young Frenchman Louis Leterrier was promoted to sole director while Corey Yuen focused on martial arts choreography.

Interviewed on the set of *Transporter 2*, Jason revealed 'We always thought that if the first one performed well we'd make a second. But for the second we'd bring it to America. So that's why we decided to shoot in Miami.'

Having arrived in Florida, Jason recalled Luc Besson's appearance at the new film's location: 'He came to Miami and we sat in a hotel room and put out chairs as if we sat in a car and we acted out the scenes … What was Frank gonna do? Was he gonna continue to be a transporter or not? When we see him here in Miami we don't really know what he's doing. He's not really transporting, he's just filling in for a friend … Then all of a sudden the trouble finds him.'

Transporter 2 started in exactly the same way as the first film, with Frank Martin in the driving seat (although the BMW had been traded in for a souped-up Audi), waiting in a multi-storey car park, mentally preparing for his next job. The opening scenes again set the tone as Frank – the meticulously organised loner – removed and folded his freshly laundered jacket before disarming a gang of would-be car-jackers.

Initially, it looked as if Frank has given up his dangerous transporting career for a safer, quieter job as a chauffeur, ferrying a little rich kid to and from school. But the kid turned out to be the son of a top politician who's battling against mafia drug dealers. Before Frank knew it, the boy gets kidnapped by the bad guys and the transporter's right in the middle of a hostage-ransom and deadly-virus plot that threatened the entire planet.

Although Jason suggested that, alongside the action scenes where he 'really expressed myself physically', there was 'also a lot more story' to *Transporter 2*, in many ways Leterrier's film failed to build on the strengths of its predecessor. The CGI rarely looked convincing, too many of the stunts were comically over-the-top and some of the casting defied logic. Having appeared with Jason in *Lock Stock*, *Snatch* and *Mean Machine* didn't necessarily qualify Jason Flemyng to play the hapless Russian villain Dimitri, while Kate Nauta's role as an evil assassin-atrix dressed only in bra, pants, suspenders and high heels teetered from the initially sexy to the rudely ridiculous.

Although, generally, *Transporter 2* received positive reviews, Jason later admitted he had 'some issues with the second one'. As Laura Kern in the *New York Times* put it, 'purely shallow but never dull, the film wisely pushes the limits of absurdity to the extreme, making it easier to submit to its sheer camp'. Given that there had only been a very brief (non-naked) seduction scene in the first *Transporter* film, it hadn't seemed odd or old-fashioned when Frank rejected the sexual advances of the kidnapped boy's mother

Audrey (played by Amber Valetta) in the second.

As before, chasing the younger action hero audience, the producers had wanted a '15' certificate for the *Transporter* franchise, but the marketing campaign might have been hampered by director Louis Leterrier's comment that 'if you watch the movie and you know he (Frank Martin) is gay, it becomes so much more fun'. (Leterrier would go on to direct *The Incredible Hulk* and *Clash of the Titans*, but he wouldn't work on *Transporter 3*.)

Despite all this, *Transporter 2* made more than $15million in profit at the box office, and, somewhat reluctantly, many critics concluded that Jason Statham was the prime reason for this. Describing the actor as 'a walking breeze-block who gargles broken glass every morning', *Total Film* declared it 'a bad movie that's impossible to hate, as Statham batters hordes of inept gunmen, effortlessly dodges bullets and pulls off ludicrous stunts involving everything from Audis to jet-skis'. The *Chicago Sun Times* admired 'an ingenious plot that continues to reveal surprises and complications well into the third act' and stated that 'this is not simply a movie where the good guy chases the bad guys, but a movie where the story turns a lot trickier than we expected'. The *New York Post*, meanwhile, opined that 'the film busts the credibility meter early on, quickly becomes preposterous, then really lets its imagination rip'.

Stephen Hunter, writing in the *Washington Post* seemed to enjoy the film against his better judgement and rather cattily reflected on Jason's progress in comparison with that of his old *Lock Stock* benefactor: 'Statham isn't the best thing in *Transporter 2*; he's essentially the only thing. It's his charisma versus the world. Score: Statham 2, World nought. He's an

Englishman – balding, lithe, focused – discovered by director Guy Ritchie ... and now he's doing better than Ritchie. Plus he's not married to Madonna.'

After the great box-office business for *Transporter 2*, the offers came in thick and fast for Jason. Meaty, dramatic parts in *London*, *The Bank Job* and Guy Ritchie's *Revolver* would be interspersed with action man roles in *Chaos*, *Crank*, *War* and *Death Race*. Whereas he had appeared in four films released between 2002 and 2004, he would feature in eleven from 2005 to 2008. Whether or not it was due to the breakdown of his relationship with Kelly Brook, Jason seemed to be investing more and more of his emotional and physical energy in his work. Post-*Transporter 2*, he was in great demand and his manager's phone rarely stopped ringing.

But commercially, the fifty-million-dollar question just had to be 'When are you going to make *Transporter 3*?' 'People keep saying "When are you going to do another one?",' laughed Jason. 'Luc (Besson) wants to do another one. I want to work with Luc. You don't want to give people too much of one thing. You know, if you eat ice cream every day, you get bored of it. But Luc says he's got an amazing idea for part three, so if it's a great story I'm sure we can improve on the last one.'

Jason had first confirmed that *Transporter 3* was definitely going to happen while promoting *Revolver* back in 2005: 'Actually we're putting petrol in the car right now ... we're gonna do one next year, maybe in the early part but certainly no later than by the summer. I'm looking forward to it, ready to get back on the horse. We've actually had a lot of conversations over the last year or so, and we want to resurrect that franchise and have some fun. I've been training recently and I'm in good shape and hoping to exceed what we did on the last two. Make it even more fun, more entertaining.'

But Jason's many other commitments, not to mention Luc Besson's diverse work on *seventeen* films released in 2006 and 2007, delayed ignition of the project. It wouldn't be until Jason had completed his work on *The Bank Job* that he could confirm all systems go: 'We've got the whole crew back together. I think Luc's getting involved with this. He's got a bit of time so he's really pushing himself on the creative side. He's going to be very present because we're shooting in Paris, so he's going to keep us all under the reign of his creative side. There's nothing more appealing than that because I've watched Luc's movies millions of times. *La Femme Nikita*, *The Professional*, I love it! To have him hands-on with Cory Yuen coming in to do the action. I'm training every day. I'm already in great shape.'

'We had plenty of fun making the first two,' Jason told *Time Out*. 'The second one was pretty successful, and people made a few dollars out of it, but we didn't do it just to turn over some money. There's always the worry that, if it doesn't exceed what the last one did, in terms of popularity, we've all made a big mistake. So there's a bit of pressure, but Luc can shoulder that I'm sure.'

It said a lot about Jason's character – and his loyalty to those who had helped him – that, in the same way he had praised Guy Ritchie, he would express his lasting gratitude to the team behind *The Transporter*: 'It was great being reunited with all the people who gave me my big break in the action world: Luc Besson, Steve Chasman and Corey Yuen. If it wasn't for those guys, I wouldn't be sitting here all these years later making Part Three.'

Transporter 3 (2008) relocated Frank Martin back in France with the tag-line: 'This time the rules are the same ... except one'.

The action-film world had clearly changed in the years since the first part of the series had appeared: 'The level of action this time has been multiplied by three,' observed Jason. 'The Bourne trilogy propelled action movies into the new millennium. So with this movie we had to step up our game. Everything is bigger.'

Luc Besson, Steve Chasman, Corey Yuen and Robert Mark Kamen were all on board once again, this time along with another French action-movie director, Olivier Megaton (who had worked on the successful *Hitman* with Timothy Olyphant), plus an untried Russian actress.

'Luc Besson thought he had the best script of all three and told me he'd found this new girl, Natalya Rudakova, on the streets, literally, who'd be perfect,' said Jason. 'She used to be a hairdresser; an amazing chick hand-picked by the man himself. She's never acted, she's just completely fresh. I think he has an amazing skill to pick great girls like Milla Jovovich and Natalie Portman.'

Rudakova would play Jason's love interest in the film. 'She's really crazy like a lot of modern young girls,' she said. 'As the only female character in the movie, she brings spontaneity and spice to the picture. She's a real volcano.'

Also involved – for the third time in the franchise – was François Berléand as Tarconi, the French policeman who always turned to assist Frank Martin. Berléand spoke fondly of being reunited with his good friend Jason: 'We fall into each other's arms every time.'

The complicated plot of *Transporter 3* found Frank Martin

reluctantly becoming a driver-for-hire once again. This time he had to drive a kidnapped Ukrainian girl named Valentina (the flame-haired Rudakova) from Marseilles to Odessa so that her politician father – the head of the Ukrainian environmental agency – would sign policy documents preventing environmental reforms, thereby allowing unprincipled American chemical companies to dump hazardous waste in his country.

The tension was heightened by the fact that Frank's 'employers' had fitted him with an explosive bracelet that would detonate if he moved more than 100 feet from his car. Plus, along the way, love and lust blossom when Valentina forced Frank into an open-air striptease to recover the keys to his beloved Audi – this sequence became a huge hit on YouTube – and, at last, our hero got the girl. Or she gets him.

'I think in the third film, we've found his weakness,' Jason said of Frank's latest reincarnation, 'which lies in the lovely female he's with. Obviously, there's the challenge of how to make things more interesting, how to make Frank more interesting, and how to exceed what's happened in the first two films. There's a lot to live up to with the character. Hopefully, we've made this one interesting enough.'

'Jason Statham – super-ripped, bullet-headed and expression adjusted to Perma-Scowl – reprises his role as the world's studliest deliveryman,' trumpeted *Village Voice*. 'But here's what all fans need to know: yes, Statham strips to the waist multiple times . . .'

By now he had become famous as 'The Stath', the body-beautiful, the ultimate macho white fighting machine. All the typical Jason Statham martial-artist-meets-action-man stunts were once again present and correct, including a fantastic sequence in which he was forced to race his own Audi on a bicycle. But it was the unexpected development in Frank Martin's emotional make-up that really set *Transporter 3* apart from its predecessors.

'When he was unattached, Frank was just a cool machine,' said director Olivier Megaton. 'In love, he's much more vulnerable. He allows himself to express emotion and, above all, he refuses to leave Valentina at the side of the road to save his own skin. The stakes are raised, which adds a new dimension to the character.'

Jason would agree with this explanation. While he clearly relished this further complex and emotional twist in the evolution of Frank Martin's character, he fully understood the increased danger it placed him in: 'This woman comes along and really upsets the apple cart. If you live a certain way, you're protected. But once you integrate something that comes with an emotional bag, then everything gets upset and you can't function properly. That's why some military guys have a certain regime that they like to stick to. They don't have their wives close to them. They have a solitary existence, a protected existence. When you have someone who you care about very deeply, it affects your mindset.'

This statement encouraged one journalist to bravely ask him if there were any similarities between Frank's character and Jason's own. In response, Jason laughed and parried away the comparison: 'I like his suits, I like the style of him, but he's a character created by Luc Besson. He's a very internal guy, I'm not. I'm a little bit more expressive and I like a bit of fun.'

Jason as Frank, the lover and the fighter, clearly had plenty of fun on *Transporter 3*. Many reviewers raved about the stunts and special effects, although, as one boffin suggested, it was 'completely unbelievable in terms of logic, mechanics and physics'. Leslie C. Halpern, writing for Suite101.com, wrote that 'having lost weight and pumped up his torso for the role of Frank, Statham jumps on a bicycle, single-handedly fights a room full of killers, drives on top of a train and does some underwater magic in order to save himself and Valentina from their seemingly unavoidable fate'.

Despite being the most entertaining and action-packed movie of the franchise – 'it's the charismatic unruffled dexterity in the face of impossible odds that rivets,' wrote Christopher Borelli in the *Chicago Tribune* – *Transporter 3* surprisingly failed to repeat the profitable success of *Transporter 2*, casting doubts on the further future of the brand.

It remains to be seen whether Frank Martin will ride again or whether he will finally be able to go fishing, peacefully, until the end of his days. If the latter proved to be true, then surely Jason Statham – the best English Hollywood action hero since Roger Moore – would always have affectionate memories of the character's starring role in his own professional journey onto Hollywood's A-list.

Reflecting on the *Transporter* series Jason once said, 'Luc [Besson] is ultimately responsible for the creation of the character ... and frankly for me being here in Hollywood right now. If it weren't for the first *Transporter* film, I wouldn't be in this position. It was the first movie I did where I had the lead, and certainly the first action movie I'd ever done. It takes a lot of balls to gamble on somebody like me – somebody who didn't have a resume to back himself up. I'm grateful to have had a chance like that.'

CHAPTER SIX:

FIGHTING FIT

In Hollywood terms, this would be the major question surrounding Jason Statham and the future direction of his career. Could the inexperienced Englishman, with his shaved head, menacing scowl and gravel tones – an actor who had only been in a handful of films – possibly be the salvation of American action-adventure movies?

By the close of the 20th century, the big-budget blockbusters – fronted by brickhouse-built macho heroes – seemed to have died a death. The key players seemed to be heading for their pensions or politics or losing their commercial advantage. New pretenders such as Vin Diesel, Wesley Snipes, and Dwayne 'The Rock' Johnson had somehow failed to build on the successes of their early films and capture the imagination of the next generation of cinema-goers. The only major area of growth in terms of action movies appeared to be in the Asian martial arts industry, fronted by Jackie Chan and Jet Li.

Other factors also acted against the old-style genre. Politically, the Cold War had ended and the traditional former enemies in the Soviet Union and the Far East – antagonists in every battling blockbuster from the Bond films to *Rambo* – were being replaced by more sinister, extreme, complex and evasive forces such as Al-Qaeda in Iraq and Afghanistan.

Following September 11th, 2001, and the subsequent loss of so many young soldiers in foreign fields trying to stem the further threat of international terrorism, such subject matter would be regarded as too painful, too sensitive for Hollywood to tackle in the name of entertainment. As a result, early 21st-century audiences were more attracted to escapist, tongue-in-cheek period adventure productions such as *Pirates of the Caribbean*, starring the anti-macho, almost-feminine Johnny Depp as Jack Sparrow.

The few, big-budget, action-entertainment films that were being made at the dawn of the new millennium – mainstream martial arts movies (for example, *Crouching Tiger, Hidden Dragon*), superheroes (*The X-Men*, *Spider-Man*), classical adventures (*Gladiator*), fantasy features (*Lord of the Rings*), plus conflicts with extra-terrestrials and revivals of the gangster genre – tended to focus on old-fashioned or imagined enemies, or individual rogue villains who either wanted to blow up the world or control the flow of drugs. Also, the revolutionary development of CGI and animation meant that the major studios had started to invest their millions in very different ways (as seen in films such as *Shrek* and *Monsters, Inc.*, both 2001). Hollywood certainly didn't seem to be making films like *The Terminator*, *Die Hard*, *Raiders of the Lost Ark* or *Robocop* any more.

Perhaps modern audiences wanted more brain and less

brawn in their leading men; the pretty boys (Leonardo DiCaprio, Johnny Depp, Matt Damon) were big at the box office and both the decrepit old guard and the latest breed of action heroes started to move into film genres such as drama, comedy or even children's films (such as Dwayne Johnson appearing in the *Tooth Fairy*). Of the pretenders to Stallone and Schwarzenegger's crown, arguably Vin Diesel and Wesley Snipes would make poor choices, appearing in films that concentrated on action sequences while failing to heed the need for a strong script or a sophisticated plot.

The action-hero market has often proved to be a goldmine for Hollywood producers. In audience-targeting terms there has always been a desperate desire to get teenagers to part with their cash. Some critics claimed that the James Bond franchise had lost its sense of humour and direction and had begun to look its age – the latest incumbent Daniel Craig was more of a player than an action man – while the new Bourne brand (with Matt Damon) was more psychological and complex than all-action.

If the adventure genre desperately needed a shot in the arm – a convincing contender, a ray of hope – then it came in 2001 in the form of Jason Statham. His work in Guy Ritchie's *Lock Stock ...* and *Snatch* had proved he could perform charismatically on the big screen, but the black-comedy gangster genre hadn't given him the opportunity to do more than look 'hard' and sound streetwise, albeit in a charming, loveable cockney-geezer fashion. Even though, in *Snatch*, he had played a boxing promoter, there was little evidence in the film that he could handle himself in the ring. Similarly, although they showcased him as a convincingly tough character actor, neither of his first adventures in

Hollywood – *Turn It Up* (2000) and *Ghosts of Mars* (2001) – really revealed the full range of his talents.

One wonders if there was a point, in late 1999 or early 2000, when Steve Chasman first realised the great potential of the actor he was now managing. Obviously, Chasman would have known about Statham's diving background, and 'kick-boxing skills' might have been listed on Jason's resume. Was there a small-talk conversation in which Jason suddenly revealed he had practised jiu-jitsu? Or, better still, an almost cinematic, defining moment in the gym when Chasman first witnessed the actor's martial arts abilities? Whatever the sequence of events, within months Statham would be filming *The One* alongside his hero Jet Li. From that point onwards, his transition towards action-hero status began to gain real momentum.

Jason's interest in combat sports had originally come from his family. According to the *Independent*, 'his father was a boxer and a gymnast, and taught his son both. His brother loved martial arts and used little Jason as his personal punchbag.' The thrill obviously rubbed off on young Jason, who taught himself to box when he was a teenager. Later, when Jason was interviewed about his role as a boxing promoter in *Snatch*, he'd reply: 'I'm a big boxing fan and it was something I understood.'

He'd become interested in martial arts as a kid – in his late teens he'd take up kick-boxing at a gym in London's Shoreditch – and would often express his passion and admiration for the stars of the classic kung fu film genre from the 1970s and 1980s. 'I'm impressed with the likes of Jet Li and Jackie Chan, and Bruce Lee was a big hero of mine for many years. They're great influences. Bruce Lee ... he's the fucking real deal, you know? Most of the Asian action stars have been inspirational to me: Jet Li, Jackie Chan, Tony Jaa – they're fucking great at what they do and *it is them doing it*. They impress me, not people who take credit for something they don't do.'

The early realisation that these great martial artists were doing their own stunts in their own films would clearly have a lasting effect on Jason's own career. Although later, when he was asked what level of martial artist he was, he modestly replied 'movie level', he would spend the early years before his film career started, practising different disciplines.

'I've fucked around at all kinds of martial arts really ... kick-boxing, wing chun, jiu-jitsu and a bit of judo with Guy Ritchie. And I've fannied around with various other forms. But obviously the style used in the movies isn't a practical one for actual combat. The movie style of fighting is completely exaggerated with over-the-top movements. You'd get completely hammered if you fought like that in a real fight situation.'

Arguably the biggest single influence on Jason's early action-hero film career would be martial arts legend Jet Li, who had studied Chinese martial arts (wushu) from the age of eight and reigned as National Wushu Champion of All China from 1974 to 1978. In 1974, at the height of the Watergate scandal and when peace had broken out between the USA and China, Jet Li had performed in the Rose Garden of the White House for President Nixon.

Jet Li and the martial arts choreographer Corey Yuen were both managed by Ace Media's Steve Chasman. As an actor, Yuen had worked in many of the great kung fu films of the 1970s and 1980s, including 1972's *Fist of Fury* with Bruce

Lee (and a young Jackie Chan). Together this triumvirate of Li, Yuen and Chasman would help develop Jason Statham into an international star. Another of their strong contacts would be French director and *Transporter* screenwriter Luc Besson, who in 2000 was working with Yuen and Li on *Kiss of the Dragon* (a film produced by Chasman).

The high level of respect between Jet Li, Corey Yuen and Jason was completely mutual; *The One* would be the first of three films Jason made with them during the 2000s, including *War* (a.k.a. *Rogue*) in 2006 and *The Expendables* in 2010. The experience of working with these seasoned martial arts masters further encouraged his interest in different disciplines of the sport.

While filming with his competitive friend and director Guy Ritchie, he would regularly practise both judo and karate, often at the Budokwai centre for martial arts in Chelsea. 'Guy puts in more hours than me,' admitted Jason. 'So he's got the edge. He's a third dan shotokan black belt. There was a time we were evenly matched. If I devoted every day to it, I could have him.'

Did they give each other black eyes? 'No black eyes, but we give each other a serious change of colour; arm bars, knee bars, toe holds, chokes, they're the main things.'

Some martial arts observers who have studied Jason's kick-boxing techniques (particularly in the *Transporter* and *Crank* films) read much deeper into their origins and influences. They suggest his action style is similar to *savate* or *boxe française*, the 19th-century French art of street fighting with hands and feet ('savate' means 'old shoe'), offering a multi-discipline improvised approach to personal combat.

Jason has also talked on several occasions about his

passion for Brazilian jiu-jitsu, which uses the principle of leverage to attack the two weakest parts of the body – the joints and the arteries. Interestingly, many serious practitioners also favour Brazilian jiu-jitsu because of its emphasis on chess-style mental strategies. It's this combination of mental and physical techniques that attracts UFC (Ultimate Fighting Competition) competitors to the discipline.

'That is by far my favourite sport,' Jason has said of UFC, 'the only thing that holds my attention. I go to all the matches, I have respect for those guys above all other athletes. They are the ultimate. It takes elements from judo, jiu-jitsu, kick-boxing and you use every part of what is usable in a real fight situation. In its early days it used to be a kung fu champion against a wrestling champion. The best man or the best art would win. I like to watch it. It's pretty violent. You are fighting to knock someone out or put them in a submission, but I've never done that.'

After being spotted at UFC 100 in Las Vegas in 2009, Jason was asked if he'd considered becoming one of the modern gladiators in Ultimate Fighting Competition. 'I've become a big fan,' he replied, 'but the thought of me stepping into the Octagon with somebody like Chuck Liddell actually frightens me because those guys are lethal.'

While on location in Brazil, filming *The Expendables* in 2009, Jason commented: 'Brazil is a place I'd been looking to go to for a long, long time. You know I've got a particular fascination with jiu-jitsu and some of the best fighters in the world are down here in Brazil. We went to a great gym four or five nights ago. Antônio Rodrigo Nogueira, 'Minotauro', we went to his gym and he put on a few fights for us. It was terrific, what a great time!'

Alongside Jason and Nogueira (a former UFC heavyweight champion), several other members of *The Expendables*' cast were also practitioners of Brazilian jiu-jitsu, including Mickey Rourke and Steve Austin. One of the sport's greatest exponents, the Filipino-American Dan Inosanto, worked closely with Bruce Lee on *The Game of Death* (1978) and later appeared in *Big Trouble in Little China* (1986) and Steven Seagal's *Out of Justice* (1991).

Looking back over Jason's career as a martial artist in the movies, and studying his interviews on this subject, it becomes clear that his passion for the sport goes much deeper than the theatrical combat elements. Aside from the obvious career and commercial benefits that his martial arts talents have generated – and the contribution his study of various disciplines has made to his high level of physical fitness – he's always been interested in the philosophy behind the fighting.

When, during an interview with Jeffrey Lyons on the American TV show *Reel Talk*, it was suggested that his martial arts movies might have a negative influence on younger members of his audience, Jason replied: 'Any martial art or discipline of that nature actually breeds a bit of peace. It's the people who don't have the discipline who are causing stinks or fights with people. You find that any of the guys that have a certain skill within that fighting world – whether it be judo, kick-boxing, Thai boxing, jiu-jitsu – they're very peaceful people. And the only aggression they have time for is in a competition environment.'

In 2000, however, Jason's first journey into the martial arts genre hadn't worked out quite as planned. In *The One*, the sci-fi plot was over-complicated: the many different personalities portrayed by Jet Li meant that there was greater dependence on stuntmen and face-replacement techniques achieved with computer graphics. The 'behind-the-scenes' feature of *The One* DVD offered a greater indication of Jet Li's talents filmed simply against the green screen, before the CGI was keyed in during post-production.

In *The One*, Jason's own martial arts stunts were limited by time restrictions and other commitments, but he was full of praise for his hero Jet Li. 'He's significantly gifted, he's a unique individual. Martial arts isn't just about physicality. As he said, it's the spirit and the mind and that breeds – if you keep practising this kind of thing in your life – an inner confidence and knowledge through life and people and the world around you. You can't help but listen to the man. He ain't like Tom, Dick and Harry down the street getting drunk. He's an interesting man ... a very funny guy. He cracks me up all the time.'

His experience working on *The One* also taught Jason some very hard lessons about physical preparations for martial arts movies; lessons he would remember throughout his future career. 'We did a few rehearsals in the first week and I was totally out of shape. The fight training was very extensive, a lot of stretching, a lot of co-ordination of balance exercises. I had a twisted neck and a sprained knee, they really put me through the paces.'

It became crystal-clear to Jason that even he – a former world-class diver and dedicated athlete – would need to work harder at getting fitter and stronger to sustain a long-term career in martial arts and action movies.

Jason's previous life as a sportsman had taught him how to focus on forthcoming competitions, but he admitted (with hindsight) that after becoming a film actor he'd turned a bit 'lardy'. For years he'd eaten and drunk what he liked – 'I was drinking and shagging a lot' – but, once in Hollywood, his target would be to achieve ultimate fitness ahead of filming.

'You have to lead a different lifestyle,' he'd observe later in his career. 'You have to be extreme. You go to bed early because you get up early ... you're locked in, focused ... that's how you get results quick. It's like being in a professional sport.'

He radically changed his diet, dumping the bacon sandwiches and pizzas for a strict 2,000-calories-maximum-per-day regime, avoiding bread, pasta, sweets, fruit juices and, above all, booze; 'that's the hardest part right there'. Instead of three square meals each day he'd now eat six small meals featuring egg whites, lean meats, fish, vegetables, protein shakes and nuts, plain yoghurt with fresh fruit: 'It's like being in prison,' he grumbled. 'Fucking salmon and broccoli, salmon and broccoli! I never gave a fuck about a calorie. An apple? It's good for me. I'd have five. Bananas? Eat the bunch!'

Once, when he was asked what he'd eaten in order to lose 17lb (7.7kg) in only six weeks, he replied: 'Not much. Mainly protein, nuts and berries. I was a miserable bastard.'

Nevertheless, such was his focus and self-discipline, he carried a little black book with him everywhere he went, detailing everything he swallowed, including the one-and-a-half gallons of water he'd routinely drink every day. 'If you want to get faster, stronger and healthier you have to record and track your progress. Making progress is the primary goal of the training I've been doing.'

It sounded as if he found abstinence from alcohol one of the toughest elements of his training regime: 'I had a four-month spell when I'd gone to train for *Death Race* in Canada and I never touched a single beer. There was no alcohol ... that was the cleanest I've ever been. You'd have people going out and they'd say, "Come on, just come and have a beer". There's a weakness there because I come from England, but I wanted to try and stay on the tracks. I wanted to work really hard at what I had disciplined myself to do.'

However, as he later confessed to Chrissy Iley of the *Sunday Times*, he was only human and, once filming was over, there had been inevitable lapses in his commitment to achieving the total action man physique: 'I go from super-healthy to super unhealthy, with excessive drinking. When I come home and catch up with friends, that involves going down the boozer and a fair amount of pints disappear down my gullet.'

This zealous drive towards – and focus on – ultimate health and fitness would set him apart from his competitors in the adventure-hero stakes. Some of his training tips might sound common sense and obvious. 'Train early in the morning, get out of bed and just do it ... that way you'll never find an excuse not to.' Or 'get serious, do forty hard minutes not an hour and a half of nonsense, it's so much more rewarding'. But his now-legendary fitness programmes would have interviewers and observers gasping in out-of-breath disbelief and imagined agony.

Jason would sometimes train at 87 Eleven, the action-film company and stunt studio near Los Angeles airport. Owned and run by Hollywood stuntmen, the facility offered everything from trampolines, crash pads, kettlebells and heavy bags through to climbing ropes, rowing machines and medicine balls.

His martial arts work-out might initially involve shadow-boxing to loosen up the back and shoulders, and warming up by lunging and stretching the legs. These exercises could be followed by five three-minute rounds of punching and kicking pads, then three more rounds of hitting a heavy bag, before another session on a speed bag.

The ten-minute warm-up (generally cardio work such as rowing) would be followed by ten minutes at medium intensity (press-ups and circuit training) preparing for the brutal final stage that, in his own words, 'blows every gasket . . . you're crying for air. It redlines the heart into oblivion.'

Another typical routine might include 500 sit-up variations every day, ten minutes of rowing, a 40kg rope pull (the rope would be attached to a weighted sled), snatch grip dead lifts (five at 45kg, five at 60kg, five at 95kg), abdominal roll-outs, triceps extensions, dumbbell bench-presses, standing military presses, skull-crushers, Bulgarian split squats, hanging knee raises . . .

'I trained six days a week, thirty-five minutes a day,' he'd tell *Men's Fitness Magazine*. 'We had two rules: we wouldn't do the same work-out twice and we'd record everything. The main part of the session would be intense and involve heavy compound lifts, circuits, kettlebells and medicine balls.' Yet he'd also declare that he wasn't interested in weightlifting simply for appearance's sake: 'Muscle men grow on trees. They can tense their muscles and look good in a mirror. So what? I'm more interested in practical strength that's going to help me run, jump, twist, punch.'

Generally it seemed Jason would avoid using gym equipment, preferring hard, fast circuits involving skipping, squat thrusts, star jumps, push-ups, tuck jumps and step-ups followed by punching combinations based on advice from his good friend, the Dutch mixed martial artist and UFC legend

Sebastiaan 'Bas' Rutten. On Saturdays, Jason would do an hour-long sustained trail run through the Hollywood Hills.

Interestingly, his anti-equipment attitude had been inspired by a visit to California's Corcoran State Prison. He'd watched the inmates achieve 'prison shape' fitness as opposed to 'gym shape' fitness. 'They had banned weights from the prison yard,' he explained to journalist Karl Greenfield. 'They didn't have the big, fat machines you have in a typical gym. These guys were using their own bodies for lifts, pull-ups, sit-ups and squats. They employed full-body-weight exercises and old-school gym techniques that seemed to work wonders.'*

By his own admission he had always avoided Hollywood-style personal trainers – 'You see people working out with some trainers and the trainers look like they need trainers ... it's bizarre how they get the job if they're not in amazing fucking shape themselves' – until he started to work out with the former Navy SEAL Logan Hood to achieve peak condition ahead of filming *Death Race* in 2007.

Hood, who runs Epoch Training in Inglewood, Los Angeles, and who had also trained Jason's friend and colleague Vinnie Jones, only agreed to take on actors who were totally committed to getting and *staying* fit. Confronted with most celebrities, Hood commented, 'I can look in their eyes and see if

---

* One of Jason's encounters on his visit to Corcoran Prison was memorable for a very different reason. As director Paul W. S. Anderson explained, 'We met this mass murderer who had done a number of decapitations on the outside, and several on the inside too. He was one mean motherfucker and he came up to the window with these really dark murderous eyes and said, "You know who you look like? Jason Statham!" We all went, "Fuck, how the hell did he know that?"'

they're full of shit'. With Jason, he knew from day one that his new recruit was a natural, serious athlete.

Jason was once asked how long it took him to get into great shape before each feature film. 'Ten weeks is good,' he replied. 'If you can do ten weeks you can make some real changes. Anything under six weeks you may as well forget about it.' Working with Logan Hood, by the time Jason reached the set of *Death Race* he was in great condition. 'I've never had a trainer in my life, this is a whole new experience,' he would say, 'and I'm in better shape now than I've ever been.'

One interviewer around this time, Mike Zimmerman of *Celebrity Fitness*, couldn't help but agree: 'He lifts up his shirt. He's shredded – rumble-strip abs, cords in his chest, veins in his arms . . . He's in *incredible* physical condition – everything he does is forceful – and his opinions are about as strong as his handshake.' Tellingly, in terms of the self-sacrifice involved in Jason's spartan training regime, Zimmerman also added, 'if you start modelling your work-outs on his, you should know that he often refers to them as horrible, nauseating, bastard, murder, nightmare and priceless, preceding each description with the word "fucking".'

Normal, everyday Hollywood actors definitely needed to look good but, in truth, didn't need to be super-fit. Most well-paid and pampered A-listers could happily point to health and safety or insurance issues and warmly embrace the idea that – for contractual reasons – body-doubles and stuntmen could and should represent them in scenes involving even minimal risk or minor danger.

Not Jason Statham. As Simon Lewis in the *Daily Mail* pointed out about the actor, 'almost uniquely outside of

Hong Kong cinema, he does all his own stunts and fights'. This reference to Asian films is key. Growing up, watching Bruce Lee and later Jackie Chan, and working with Jet Li, Jason had realised that in order to be accepted as a convincing and respected action star, the audience needed to believe in him as an athlete, a character actor *and* as a martial artist.

'To me it's a very balletic kind of choreography that they do,' he said of his martial arts heroes. 'I'm used to, like, street-brawling and punching a bag until you're black and blue, whereas this is a much more graceful and stylised way of fighting. It stands out. It's fantastic! You know they are the best of the best and it's great to be with them.'

One of his female co-stars, Amber Valetta (who played the love interest Audrey in *Transporter 2*), also noted the influence of Hong Kong cinema and choreography on Jason when she witnessed him in action on set: 'Watching him doing the fight scenes was like watching a dancer. I was pleasantly surprised by him and his abilities to act and also do all the technical manoeuvring, the stunts and stuff.'

'Jason can really do these things,' Steve Chasman would happily explain (sounding like a man who'd found the pot of gold at the end of the rainbow). 'He's really athletic, he's a great driver. We can put him in situations where the audience knows this guy's *really* doing it.'

Although Jason would learn a lot about physical preparation for fights and stunts through working on *The One* with Jet Li, the greatest challenge would be his first leading action role as Frank Martin in 2002. It was an experience he'd look back on with huge affection: 'As a kid I wanted to be like a stuntman, throw myself around and pick myself up, but I never kind of fulfilled that. I went years and years without even pursuing that any further and then, a few years ago, I had the chance to do it in *The Transporter*.'

The Transporter had showcased his many different skills perfectly, in action-packed sequences such as car chases, scuba-diving stunts and, particularly, martial arts routines. Apart from introducing him as a new, youthful face to action-adventure audiences, the film confirmed Jason as a charismatic all-round talent; a rugged-looking man of few words, who could out-think and out-manoeuvre the villains, coolly make the right decisions in dangerous situations, and bravely protect the beautiful-but-vulnerable girl. In sections of the American press he was instantly hailed as the man most likely to replace Chuck Norris as 'Hollywood's most dangerous white boy'.

'The best fight scenes are always the ones that are most realistic,' Jason would say. 'There are lots of movies you see now where you don't know who's doing what. It could be my grandma ... a lot of actors can't do their fights so they have to disguise it in some way, so they use tight angles and fast cuts.' Like his screen idol Bruce Lee, Jason favoured wide-angle shots that revealed his fighting skills: 'No wires, no flying around, no exaggerated fancy movements. So I think you'll see what we're doing is very realistic.'

Although the common view in Hollywood would be that bigger-budget films produce better action-adventure sequences, Jason was of a different opinion: 'When you only have certain resources at your fingertips it can make you a little more creative because you have to be. James Bond cost $220million, for instance, so basically there's no limit to what they can do. We ain't got the money to do that [*The Transporter* cost a tenth of the Bond budget] so we have to

115

do it for real and shoot it through the camera because we can't say, "We can sort that out with CGI". In my book, it's infinitely better anyway. It looks more realistic and you can have some fun doing the stunts.'

Typically, despite the praise heaped on him for his newly acquired action-hero status, Jason knew that this was just the beginning and that, with determination, he could and would do better. 'It was my first attempt at that kind of physical role, and I think I learned so much from that. I think that whatever I do next along those lines, you know, will certainly exceed what I did in *The Transporter*. And I'm very much looking forward to that.'

The second *Transporter* film raised the action stakes higher, as Frank Martin battled against kidnappers and tried to defeat enemies intent on spreading disease through a deadly virus. In one of the most memorable action scenes, Jason had to jump from a skidding jet-ski onto the back of a school bus. It may have appeared ridiculous in an age obsessed with health and safety in the workplace but, true to form, the leading man decided to perform the stunt himself: 'It's difficult with the stunts because we have to try and improve on what's been done before and find something you haven't already seen. It wouldn't be possible to do if you didn't have some kind of adrenaline coursing through your veins. It's better to get it in the first take or two if you can, so it's best to just switch on and be plugged into that mentally. Obviously, if we've done enough rehearsal, then we get it right.'

He got it right but later revealed that he'd had serious reservations about the stunt. The jet-ski had been fixed to a cable that ran under the moving school bus and was being pulled by a car driven in front of the bus. Crucially, for the

Jason and Guy Ritchie playing chess – a tense and competitive contest both
on and off set – during the complex and psychological film *Revolver*.

Above: Terry Leather (Jason) and old flame Martine (Saffron Burrows) in *The Bank Job*.

Opposite: Keeping the adrenaline pumping – Jason as Chev Chelios in *Crank*.

Jason poses for the hordes of paparazzi at the UK premiere of *The Bank Job*.

Above: Celebrating with Mickey Rourke and Ray Winstone after a screening of *The Wrestler*.

Opposite: Posing for a photo at the Cannes Film Festival in 2007.

With mates Vinnie Jones and Rick Hoffman at the Soccer for Survivors game in Beverly Hills.

Jason stars in the ultimate boy-racer movie *Death Race*.

Same rules, different package. Frank Martin makes a welcome comeback in

stunt to work, the driver of the car needed to gauge the speed of the bus, blindly calculate when the jet-ski would be close enough for Jason to attempt the jump, and then brake. Due to unforeseen circumstances, the stunt proved more dangerous than it should have been because certain safety gear hadn't been available. 'If the guy in front would have put on the brakes at the wrong time, I would have made the jump and hit that street. That would have been the end of me, curtains!'

For Jason and the production team behind all three *Transporter* films, there would always be a struggle to balance the levels of realism and believability in the plot against the demands for bigger, better, more outrageous stunts. As the *Los Angeles Times* once suggested, 'Like Jackie Chan, Statham has a highlight reel of over-the-top scenes where he uses not just swords and guns as weapons but nutty objects such as paint buckets, fruit, handcuffs and, most famously, a fire hose to vanquish his foes. Chan gets away with it by playing a cartoon with a bewildered grin; Statham pulls it off with that scowl and an expression of barely contained exasperation.'

One of the scenes in *Transporter 2* definitely qualified as 'over-the-top'. Knowing there was a bomb attached to the bottom of his beloved Audi, Frank Martin deliberately spins the car airborne and upside down so that the hook of a convenient crane plucks the bomb from his undercarriage just before it explodes. It was great entertainment but Jason had been less enthusiastic about the far-fetched nature of the scene: 'There are certain things that I've said "Oh God, do we really have to put that in the movie?" but my taste doesn't necessarily reflect everyone else's taste. Sometimes that kind of stuff doesn't really ring my bell.'

Transporter 3 was even less crazy and less reliant on CGI than the second film, while still featuring some fantastic – if slightly unbelievable – stunts. Arguably, the *T3* director, Olivier Megaton, succeeded where his *T2* predecessor Louis Leterrier had failed. Or perhaps, in this instance, the bigger budget helped. Certainly the fight sequences involving Jason were brilliantly choreographed by Corey Yuen.

Time Out magazine asked him about one particular *Transporter 3* scene in which he single-handedly defeated a gang of thugs in a garage. 'That was just a location problem,' he laughed. 'It was pretty tight, but we worked around it. Ideally we'd have liked to build that set and give ourselves more space to work in. When that fight was planned, there was going to be something like eighteen guys, but we had to cut it down to ten because it was just too unrealistic. But it's still a lot of people in not a lot of space with props flying all round the place.'

Amusingly, the *Time Out* writer sounded genuinely shocked and disappointed after being told that they had not been fighting with real tools. 'Of course not,' replied Jason, 'one silly mistake with a 30lb spanner and it's hospital food for anyone on the receiving end of that.'

After the first *Transporter* film, Chinese whispers had spread through Hollywood about the extraordinary Englishman who could act tough and fearlessly perform all of his own stunts. On the set of *The Italian Job* – alongside Mark Wahlberg and Charlize Theron – he would further enhance this reputation by doing all his own driving sequences. Such was Jason's commitment to the art of screen driving that he even took tuition from the former Formula One world champion Damon Hill.

There would be no substitute for hard work and intense

practice. Years later, when asked how he'd managed to become such a great driver at break-neck speed, he answered directly, 'because I did a substantial amount of training for *Death Race* and the *Transporters*, three of those fuckers now. I've put in a lot of hours behind the wheel with a lot of stunt teams, so every time I do a new movie I learn a new skill.'

A good example of his newly acquired skills would be visible in the opening action in *The Italian Job*, which involved a cleverly choreographed boating stunt with Jason at the helm. Typically, he'd stepped up to the challenge, rather than allowing a stunt driver to step into his deck shoes. But he admitted his boat-driving skills had been, by his own high standards, below par.

'It's a Boston Whaler I was driving. It's more of a fishing boat, so it's not got that much of a responsive action. But I had the confidence to get in the boat and do it. And, you know, it was under the bridges and we were making big turns in the Grand Canal. It takes seven rotations of the wheel to make the engine to go from one side to the other. So you're doing a lot of spinning and turning for not a lot of movement on the back end. And when you want to stop you can't stop. There's about fifty feet of coasting before you come to anything like a stop. It's quite worrying in that respect. It's not like you can just slam on the brakes and go "that was close". That was one of the toughest moments, the boat driving. But still it was a lot of fun.'

The continuous quest for bigger, better, more entertaining and more extreme action sequences would reach yet greater heights in 2005 when Jason started filming the *Crank* movies. His character, the assassin Chev Chelios, had been infected with a deadly poison. The only way Chev could stop the venom from killing him was by keeping his adrenaline levels incredibly high. As a result, the tempo of the storyline and the outrageousness of the stunts would be dramatically increased (even more so in the sequel, *Crank: High Voltage*).

'*Crank* is a different kettle of fish altogether,' Jason observed. 'That was equally as challenging as anything I've ever done. I'm doing crazy stunts in that. I'm hanging out of helicopters. I really risk my family allowance.'

In one scene, Jason was riding through Los Angeles at high speed on a motorbike dressed only in a hospital gown. In another he was filmed falling backwards from 200 feet with the fearlessness of a former high-diver. Then there was the truly extraordinary sequence in which he was clearly seen dangling from a helicopter, 3,000 feet above downtown LA.

'There's almost nothing but a thin piece of wire keeping me up. Even if you only slip, you smash your head against the helicopter. So many consequences, your legs are shaking. But there's nothing more rewarding. That's why I did diving for ten years, standing on the edge of the board up there with three-and-a-half spins to do before you hit the water.'

If you wondered why on earth he had agreed to do these stunts, then there were plenty of answers in his press interviews around this time. In *Maxim* magazine, for example, he compared the adrenaline-fixes Chev Chelios needed to survive with his own action-packed life, although he would admit that the energy drink Red Bull rather than pure adrenaline had helped him keep him going during filming.

Jason also talked about his own addiction to dangerous action sequences, revealing that 'there's something about the adrenaline rush of doing a stunt, testing yourself, putting yourself under that type of pressure ... You have to commit completely to what you're doing otherwise there are horrendous consequences. You could die.' But when asked if he had done the stunts because he had no fear, he countered, 'It's because you're afraid that you do it. It's about mastering the nerves and trying to turn that into confidence.'

Now that Jason had established himself as a leading action star – proving the point that, uniquely, he could and would perform all of his own stunts – some of his colleagues felt that it was perhaps time for him to settle for safety first, and let body-doubles and stunt specialists take his place in more difficult and dangerous situations. Although, frankly, this was not Jason's style, he was nevertheless always unselfishly considerate and cautious when it came to the safety of his co-stars.

As Amy Smart, who worked with him on *Crank*, confirmed, 'Jason was very protective – almost like an older brother – because he wanted to make sure I felt protected and I felt comfortable and I felt safe. We made sure with the stunt co-ordinators that I really got down all my moves in order to be safe about it. He was just very protective. He just wanted to make sure I didn't hurt myself.'

Even in his late thirties, Jason remained totally committed to being *seen* to be at the heart of the action. 'We do all of them,' he'd say in 2010 of the stunts in *The Expendables*, 'really as much as they allow me to do. All the stunts we do are shot in-camera. There's hardly a smidgen of CG. A lot of the stunts are very well thought out and we prep them so they're nice and safe and we do the scenes ourselves; real men doing real action. That's the reason they hire me, because they get their money's worth.'

Perhaps there was an early credit-crunch business reason

for his growing appeal; the idea you could cut production costs by hiring a real action hero instead of also having to employ a similarly built stuntman, stick him through make-up and then shoot him from a distance to deceive audiences. As Jason once joked, after filming *Transporter 3* in Paris, 'It's different over there in France. They can't afford a stunt double. It means another mouth to feed, more wages to pay, so you end up doing your own thing ... so now they expect me to do my own stunts.'

More seriously, as his daredevil reputation preceded him throughout Hollywood and beyond, Jason seemed to wonder if his stuntman CV might become a burden he would find hard to live down. Maybe, as he grew older and wiser, he was worried that his braveheart commitment to onscreen realism might prematurely terminate his brilliant career.

'I've sort of dug my own grave there. It was a stupid thing for me to say years ago, "Yeah I'll do all my own stunts!" Then it became, "Oh dear, I suppose I've got to do it again now." So now I do have to keep proving to myself and the public that it is me in the middle of the action. And I have a long catalogue of injuries that I won't bore you with to prove it.'

His military-style fitness regime, in tandem with the risk-taking action-packed sequences he so relished participating in, inevitably resulted in more than cuts and bruises. However much preparation went into each stunt – however well choreographed each routine might be – accidents could, and inevitably did, still happen.

'I've smashed myself around, been on crutches and broken a couple of bones, sure,' he told *Men's Fitness*. 'The most frustrating thing about injuries is that they take so bloody long to heal. I did my ankle in almost two years ago and it's never healed. I'm still suffering, then I had my cartilage removed, and then my meniscus cartilage ripped and I had this bloody bad knee. Every time I run it swells up. It's a nightmare. The thing about getting older is you don't heal very well. When you're eighteen you tear a muscle and it heals quickly, but now it takes fucking months.'

Sometimes there would be minor but irritating physical problems on set. On *Transporter 3*, for example, he had a nasty groin strain. Also, in the same film, during a fight sequence with the Dutch kick-boxing world champion Semmy Schilt, Jason recalled Schilt 'hoofing me once in the chest, it must have been five per cent of his capability, and I went flying. My feet came off the ground.' Later, during a crunching fight sequence in *Crank*, his stuntman opponent had to be taken to hospital with mild concussion.

Given the dangerous stunts he'd attempted throughout the first decade of his action-hero career, such small setbacks would be few and far between. His early experiences working with great martial artists and choreographers such as Jet Li and Corey Yuen had taught him *not* to take risks with immature opponents; to only train with people who were better than him, who had nothing to prove and wouldn't do anything stupid. 'I'm trying to sustain a career in front of the camera, so I don't want to come out with cauliflower ears. It's usually inexperienced people who don't know their capabilities that can get stupid.'

Although he had developed this great reputation as an action hero who performed his own stunts, conversely – as Jason became a bigger Hollywood star and his films received ever-increasing production budgets – there would also be increased pressures on him *not* to do so many of his own stunts.

Over the years, Hollywood action movies have been blighted by accident black-spots; tragic incidents in which actors, stuntmen and stuntwomen have been killed during filming. For example, Clint Carpenter died in a helicopter crash while shooting *Hired to Kill* (1989), Sonja Davis was killed after a high fall on *Vampire in Brooklyn* (1995), Harry L. O'Connor was fatally injured working on Vin Diesel's film *xXx* (2002) and, most famously, Brandon Lee – son of Bruce – was accidentally shot dead during a firearms stunt while filming *The Crow* in 1993.

But the pressure to reduce Jason's stunts wouldn't just be caused by health and safety legislation or concerns about lawsuits for negligence. The studio's greatest fear was injuries to the central character resulting in a costly delay, or, worse still, cancellation of the filming schedule.

'Yeah, it's an insurance detail,' agreed Jason. 'Basically the producers get a little nervous you're not going to turn up for the last day's filming. They have to judge whether it's going to be too dangerous to participate. I'd do more if they let me. I've never been frightened to do anything. It's always an issue of safety that sort of prevents me from doing everything. Apart from things like fire burns and stuff that's completely out of your control, I'm really keen to do any of that stuff anyway. I don't want to do anything that involves big explosions or anything that can go wrong with pyrotechnics. I like to be able to do something behind a wheel or a physical stunt, something that I am responsible for. I feel better if I made the mistake rather than anything mechanical being responsible.'

CHAPTER SEVEN:

MORE THAN AN ACTION MAN?

The arrival of the inscrutable and invincible Frank Martin as The Transporter had confirmed Jason Statham's place among the new generation of 21st-century action heroes. He had the tough-guy looks, the powerful physique, the martial arts skills, the courage and the conviction to do his own stunts, plus the likeable ability to convey the tongue-in-cheek message that it wasn't reality being shown on the screen; he wasn't taking himself *too* seriously.

Hollywood likes to pigeon-hole people – to put them in appropriate, easily labelled boxes in terms of genres such as romantic comedy, horror, sci-fi, kung fu, gangster films and so on. It had become blatantly obvious to anyone watching the first *Transporter* film that Jason could develop a highly lucrative career in action movies. He wasn't uncomfortable at being acclaimed as a new action hero, the 'British Bruce Willis', but he sounded cautious when asked if that was the path he intended to pursue: 'There's nothing wrong with it. It's nice. It's a funny title to wear, actually. It's not a label I'm trying to build. I try to mix things up and do other movies as well. I'm doing stuff that keeps me interested as much as doing the action stuff that people enjoy.'

Jason is a talented actor, who can turn his hand to most things. This is something he partly attributes to his intuition and, surprisingly, to his lack of formal theatrical training when he was younger. Rather than being hamstrung by any conventional techniques or particular, 'standard' methods of acting, Jason's approach is more instinctive. This makes his acting seem – and *feel* – more raw, passionate and natural: 'I am pretty self-confident. I've got a bit of intuition and experience behind me and can probably bring something to a role that someone from RADA can't. Plus, I've learnt a lot from actors like Jason Flemyng and Dexter Fletcher in *Lock Stock* ... who have been doing it for years. I don't think I would shy away from any role offered to me, although I do think I'd draw the line at running around in a pair of tights quoting Shakespeare.'

But this isn't to say that Jason doesn't see the value of professional training, despite being one of Guy Ritchie's protégés. If a leading role as Hamlet, Coriolanus or Romeo seemed extremely unlikely back in 2002, Jason certainly didn't rule out the possibility of studying theatre in order to develop his acting skills further: 'Some people have had years of tuition and it really shows. But there are certain people that disagree with that, too. Guy Ritchie, he thinks going to drama school is the worst thing in the world. He said it just turns people into clones and it takes away your intuition, and it teaches you technique. He says, "Why would anybody want to do that? You lose everything that's original and unique to an individual." So there are two thoughts to it. Look at someone like Edward Norton; a truly phenomenal actor. He definitely went to school and trained. And Robert De Niro. They're, like, the best actors in the world. It's definitely worth doing if you're going to achieve some kind of an ability like Robert De Niro.' So, while Jason never had any formal dramatic education of his own, he seems to have learned directly from observing some of the masters of the art. This combination of instinct, charisma and 'learning on the job' has brought real authenticity to his roles and is one of the reasons his portrayals always seem so credible.

After the cult success of *The Transporter*, concentrating on Hollywood action-hero roles would have been the obvious commercial route to develop Jason's career, but he and his manager Steve Chasman knew that it is all too easy to become typecast in Hollywood. English actors, in particular, can quickly become viewed in a limiting way and – as was the case for Hugh Grant after *Four Weddings and a Funeral* – could be forced to play the same role again and again. The same thing could have happened to Jason: how easy it would have been for him to become a victim of his own initial success, trapped in an image of his own creation. It would also have been an incredibly lucrative move, but did Jason really want to be typecast in this way so early in his career? If not, then his next choice of film role would be crucial. There seemed to be plenty of options available, including future work with Guy Ritchie and, inevitably, *Transporter 2*. But he was keen to build on the rough-diamond dramatic talents he had first revealed as part of the ensemble teams in *Lock Stock & Two Smoking Barrels* and *Snatch* and which he had also hinted at in *Ghosts of Mars* and *Turn It Up*. Whether as a likeable villain, a crime-fighting cop, an evil drug baron or as a law-enforcing 'multiverse' agent, he hadn't had to rely on his physical attributes and martial arts talents. The conviction in all his characters came through in the strength of his performances.

The Transporter had now enhanced his reputation as a leading hard-man in Hollywood, but few major casting directors knew much about Jason's streetwise acting ability. At best, entering the next stage of his incipient movie career, Jason had probably hoped for some minor roles in major films, such as the 'Airport Man' cameo (billed at sixty-first place in the credits) he would play in Michael Mann's Oscar-nominated Tom Cruise vehicle *Collateral*. Very briefly, but very much looking the part, he bumped into Cruise's character, switched suitcases and growled, 'Have a nice life.'

In Jason's case, good fortune definitely favoured the brave new boy. By 2002, Paramount Pictures was committed to re-making the classic 1969 British crime caper *The Italian Job*. Starring Michael Caine as the loveable cockney ex-con Charlie Crocker and Noël Coward as the criminal mastermind Mr Bridger, Peter Collinson's original film had also featured comedy stalwarts such as John Le Mesurier, Irene Handl and Benny Hill (as Professor Simon Peach). It was a much-loved ensemble piece in which Crocker's endearing gang of villains had set out to steal $4million of gold bullion from the Italian mafia. But it was probably best remembered for the crazy Mini Cooper car chase through the streets of Turin, followed by the ultimate cliff-hanger finale.

When news of the remake broke, many critics and movie-goers understandably feared the worst: why meddle with a classic? Even Mark Wahlberg (known for his role in *Boogie Nights*), who'd agreed to play Charlie Crocker in the new version, had reservations about Hollywood's backward-looking capacity to attempt reworks of great films, despite the fact that his recent involvement in *Planet of the Apes* had resulted in lucrative business for Twentieth Century Fox.

With a screenplay by Donna and Wayne Powers – based on the original version by Troy Kennedy Martin (famous for writing classic British TV series such as *Z-Cars* and *Edge of Darkness*) – and with Wahlberg in the starring role, the talented young video director F. Gary Gray managed to put together a fine supporting cast including Charlize Theron (Oscar winner for *Monster*), Seth Green, Edward Norton and the Golden Globe-winning Donald Sutherland (whose many fine film credits included *The Dirty Dozen*, *M*A*S*H*, *Klute* and *Don't Look Now*).

However, F. Gary Gray and his casting director Sheila Jaffe (who'd worked on *The Sopranos*) had been struggling to find the actor they needed to play the 'premier wheelman' character in the film, Handsome Rob. It was Jaffe who first suggested Jason Statham. 'I said "That's a great idea!" recalled Gray, 'because the script called for this pretty-looking Hollywood guy who gets all the women. But I didn't *want* to cast it the way it was written because it was less about the pretty boy and more about his swagger and his personality.' It seemed as though the right part had come along at just the right time for Jason. Handsome Rob would widen Jason's experience and develop a different side of his talents – for a change, he would be not just the action man.

It helped, too, that Jason was a huge fan of the original film. He already had fond memories of the 1969 version of

The Italian Job, saying that 'Oh yeah, that was a great movie! It's a classic. You know, most English people will talk very enthusiastically about it.'

It was a great opportunity to take part in a remake of a classic British film, and Jason was understandably delighted and honoured to be considered – albeit surprised by the direct way in which he was approached for the role. Usually, there would be a long, drawn-out casting and contractual process, followed by lengthy negotiations involving lawyers and agents, before someone can land a major part in a Hollywood blockbuster. In this instance, a single conversation seemed to secure the role. Jason recalled that 'Gary gave me a phone call one evening and we had a chat. And he says, "Great! You're in!" How cool is that? I don't know if he'd seen *The Transporter* but he'd been familiar with *Snatch* and *Lock Stock & Two Smoking Barrels*. People take chances every now and then, and you don't want to disappoint them. I'm very thankful to Gary for that.'

And how did he feel about being labelled 'Handsome Rob'? 'I would have preferred something a bit more funny like Ridiculous Rob,' he laughed, when asked about his character's name. 'He's a guy who has a way with women but his specialist skills are behind the wheel.'

Whereas the *Italian Job* of 1969 had focused on England and Turin, the 2003 Hollywood version journeyed from Venice and the Alps and back to Los Angeles. It still involved obscene amounts of mafia gold, but this time Charlie Crocker and his team – John Bridger (Sutherland), Lyle (Seth Green), Left Ear (Mos Def) and Handsome Rob (Jason) – were double-crossed by one of their own, evil Steve (Edward Norton), who stole the gold, murdered Bridger and left the rest for dead.

Back in Los Angeles, Crocker's gang swore revenge and recruited Bridger's safe-cracking daughter Stella (Charlize Theron) to recover the loot.

Thankfully, F. Gary Gray's version faithfully included key plot ingredients such as a perfect heist involving armoured trucks, mountains of gold and coloured Mini Coopers. The remake worked because of the strong ensemble cast, the chemistry between the diverse characters and the well choreographed dramatic action sequences in which, predictably, Jason shone.

More importantly, in terms of the development of Jason's future career, it was the first production for a while in which he *wasn't* called on to demonstrate his martial arts skills. The actor quipped that he was drawn to the role because he 'needed to let my knuckles dry', but the absence of martial combat in the part certainly didn't do his career any harm. Whether he's at the wheel of a Mini Cooper driving hell-for-leather through the subways of Los Angeles or cutting through the canals of Venice in a speedboat, he looked and acted the part. In fact, Gray sounded like Guy Ritchie when he expressed his passion for realistic action instead of CGI: 'I wanted everything to feel real and because of that the audience feel more connected.'

Aside from the great action, Jason's Handsome Rob delivered a performance of comedic, streetwise confidence that was closer to Michael Caine's Crocker in the original *Italian Job* than to the deadly serious Frank Martin of *The Transporter*. In one memorable scene with Seth Green – while Handsome Rob was seen seducing a cable girl in order to borrow her clothes and steal her truck – Green's character Lyle improvised a brilliant American-cockney impression of a Statham-style ladies' man charm offensive that made it into the finished film. But Jason hadn't known what Seth was doing at the time; he only realised later when shooting had finished and the director F. Gary Gray called him over to explain that they had left the camera and microphone running in the car. Watching the footage back with Gary, Jason recalled 'We was both asking for tissues. We was crying, we laughed so loud. It was a complete surprise. And to see the edited version, it's a great scene.'

This was not the only great scene, either. Such was Jason's charisma on screen – even in the big-box-office company of Wahlberg, Norton, Theron and Sutherland – that many critics felt the skinhead English hustler had managed to steal the movie by bringing what the *San Francisco Chronicle* called 'presence and comic flair' to the role. The *News of the World* said it was 'thrilling and exhilarating', *Total Film* called it 'a brilliant heist', *FHM* described it as 'slick, stylish and very sexy', while the *New York Times*' Stephen Holden added that 'Handsome Rob (Jason Statham), an English race-car whizz and world-class womanizer, is the driver of the getaway car and the movie's testosterone shot' in what he described as a 'sleek, ticking remake of the 1969 film'.

Favourably comparing the new version of *The Italian Job* to the remake of *Ocean's Eleven*, *Movie Magazine International* described Jason's performance as 'superb'. Clearly, he had proved to himself – and to anyone who might have doubted it – that he was a versatile actor who could bring real pace, comedy and flair to a major film, and successfully refresh a classic, even cult, movie. He had taken his chance on the greatest of stages, and his career would reach new heights from this point onwards. Despite his tremendous work in action films before and particularly afterwards, *The Italian Job* would remain one of Jason's best-loved and most successful films.

Modestly, he pointed to the quality of the script and story, to the style of direction and to the inspiring performances of his co-stars, as chief reasons for the film's success. He also spoke warmly of working with Donald Sutherland. The pair had a good relationship and Jason admired the professionalism and charisma that Donald brought to the set. Talking of his co-star, Jason said 'He's a wealth of experience and there's no substitute for that. Just the way he approaches things, it's just a confidence really, a very apparent one.' (In 2011, Jason and Donald would be reunited on-screen in another remake, *The Mechanic*.)

Aside from the positive critical reactions, and despite the expensive stunts in Venice and particularly Los Angeles – the final scene necessitated the closure of Sunset Boulevard for several days – *The Italian Job* did incredible box-office business after its release. Having been made for $60 million, it recouped twice as much in just twelve weeks and received an expanded run in American cinemas. The film is estimated to have earned more than £165million worldwide and made at least £7.5million in the UK alone. Given that Jason's fee for the picture was rumoured to be in the region of $450,000, Paramount Pictures must have been making some serious money.

Ever since *The Italian Job* was released in 2003 there have been constant 'leaks' about Paramount's lucrative plans for a complete cast reunion in a remake of the remake. Rumoured to be called *The Brazilian Job*, by 2008 Jason admitted he was becoming weary of being asked about it: 'I think someone should just erase it from the [Internet Movie] Database, save us all a problem and just put it back on there when it's fully due and ready. It's just one of those things. It's just sitting around.' But given that the first film was such a financial success, and there weren't any major creative differences on set, it must only be a matter of time before there's a remake.

*   *   *

Having made his mark as a loveable rogue and charming pin-up with Handsome Rob in *The Italian Job*, Jason would soon be making hearts and minds tremble in a very different way. Recruited by director David R. Ellis to take on the role of Ethan Greer in *Cellular* (2004), this time, rather than becoming the love interest, Jason found himself playing the hate-figure instead. Greer was a ruthless kidnapper; a 'crackerjack villain'; violent, irrational, psychotic; a bad man with few redeeming features, who would happily kill women and children if it served his evil purposes. Clearly, Ethan was a completely new character for Jason and this would be another role that would test the diversity of his acting talents.

Written by Larry Cohen, *Cellular* was a suspense-filled psychological thriller that played like a companion piece to his earlier screenplay for *Phone Booth*. Science teacher Jessica (Kim Basinger) was kidnapped by Greer and locked up in an attic. Greer smashes up her phone, coldly told Jessica her son would also be kidnapped and that they would both die unless she revealed her husband's whereabouts. Left on her own, Jessica pieced together the shattered phone and managed to make a random call to the cell phone of a surfer, Ryan (played by Chris Evans). Initially Ryan thought it was a prank call, but soon he was racing against time – and in conflict with the LAPD – as he tried to save Jessica and stop Greer. The tension is heightened by both Jessica's fear of Greer and the weakening battery of her phone.

The plot was simple, but incredibly effective. 'It's so universal,' Jason said, when asked about the idea behind the story. 'We live in a world that's so heavily laden with cell phones. It's a great idea. No matter what country this is seen in they'll be able to relate to it. Anything that keeps you on the edge of your seat is great to watch. And this has got some great actors in it. Kim Basinger just blows me away.'

There was a great onscreen negative chemistry between Statham and Basinger. While Kim managed to portray an everywoman character who was beautiful and vulnerable yet resourceful and strong, Jason brought a terrifying sense of menace and desperate cruelty to the brutally intense Greer, even while adopting an unusual cockney-meets-transatlantic accent. Interestingly, *Cellular*'s director David R. Ellis (a former stunt co-ordinator who'd previously worked on *Scarface*, *Fatal Attraction* and *Patriot Games*) revealed that some of the scenes between the two had not been worked through in advance: 'Kim did *not* want to rehearse them. She just wanted him to attack her and she would fight back. Jason's a big, really stout guy and she stepped up to the plate and gave him a run for his money.' This kind of improvisation created a real, often scary, sense of authenticity in the film's most dramatic scenes.

Cellular wasn't a huge-budget film ($25million) and it didn't generate outstanding business at the box office ($32million), but it was critically well received (the *Chicago*

Sun Times called it 'one of the year's best thrillers') and once again revealed Jason's versatility as an actor who could deliver a convincing performance alongside major Hollywood names. More importantly, perhaps, he had gained huge respect from the director, David R. Ellis, who predicted great things by proclaiming Jason's performance and professionalism: 'He just comes so well prepared. He takes great care of his body, he's just like . . . ripped. He's gonna be a huge star!'

Another very positive spin-off from *Cellular* – which had also featured both Jessica Biel and Chris Evans – was an underrated independent film called *London* (2005). Shot rather like a closely observed drama documentary, filmed around the same time as *Cellular*, and written and directed by Hunter Richards, *London* focused on the decadent lives of well-heeled loft-living New Yorkers.

It began by revealing the depths of despair to which the central character Syd (Chris Evans) has sunk after being dumped by a beautiful girl called London (Jessica Biel). Desperate to blot out his emotions and bury his loss, Syd was unsympathetically depicted as a boozer and drug-taker whose waking and sleeping hours were tormented by vivid flashbacks to his good times and sexual intimacy with London. When he accidentally discovered that she planned to leave New York and that a farewell party was being thrown for her, he jealously decided to gate-crash and confront her. But first he needed to buy more courage from a local coke dealer called Bateman – the character played by Jason.

Unlike most of the other films Jason had appeared in, the dramatic action in *London* took place over just one evening in a lavishly furnished New York loft apartment. Arriving at the party early, even before guest-of-honour London was present, Syd and Bateman stocked up with booze and locked themselves in the bathroom. Batemen pulled a framed Van Gogh print off the wall – symbolically Vincent's last painting, his suicide note, the wheat field with crows – laid it over the sink and uses the glass as a chopping surface for his cocaine supply. At various points in the proceedings, before Syd found the confidence to step out into the party and confront his ex-girlfriend, they were joined by two coke-seeking friends – Kelli Garner's Maya and Joy Bryant's Mallory.

Billed as 'one man's incredible journey of self-discovery', the focus of the film was clearly on Chris Evans' Syd. But, arguably, Hunter Richards' script only really came alive when Jason was in the frame. His Bateman is an extra-ordinary character; a repressed, impotent Englishman, divorced from a wife he couldn't satisfy sexually, who spends his working hours as a sober-looking currency trader and his troubled nights as a debauched coke-and-whisky-fuelled sadomasochist.

Hard-faced, bitter and unattractive, Bateman couldn't have been further from the performance Jason had played as Handsome Rob in *The Italian Job*. Whereas Rob had been a cockney Prince Charming, a legendary skirt-chaser and wheeler-dealer, Bateman operated at the darker end of the personality spectrum.

Despite an unnecessarily bad toupée, Jason delivered a powerful theatrical and psychological role in *London* that was as convincing as it was unpleasant. Yet he even managed to generate some pathetic sympathy for the character. Together, Chris Evans and Jason worked dangerously well together; two jealous, flawed men on the edge, drinking and doping each other into oblivion, bitterly scarred by relationship breakdowns, struggling to face up to their complex pasts and their uncertain futures.

As the tension built up in the claustrophobic drug-den of a bathroom, Syd kept demanding another shot of booze or another snort of coke before he could step outside into the small-talking, unbearably pleasant, cosmetic and stylish world of the party. When he finally did, there was an uncomfortable tension between Syd, Bateman and the other guests.

London (Jessica Biel) tried to encourage Syd to talk about their problems quietly, sensibly, outside. But when one of her friends verbally attacked Syd, he reacts angrily, causing another guest to punch him. This sent Jason's Bateman into a psychotic rage, an orgy of uncontrollable violence. More reminiscent of Vinnie Jones-style madness in *Lock Stock . . .* or *Snatch* – or of Jason himself as Greer in *Cellular* – his physical performance in *London* was far removed from the cool, self-defensive, strategic aggression he had demonstrated as Frank Martin in the *Transporter* films.

With a moving soundtrack by The Crystal Method, *London* was a beautifully shot art-house-style film that sadly suffered too closely from comparisons with the 2000 film adaptation of Bret Easton Ellis' *American Psycho* (in which Christian Bale had starred as the profoundly unpleasant Patrick Bateman). But if ever a film thoroughly deserved its '18' certificate for 'very strong language', it was *London*, and Jason's character was the chief culprit. While his co-stars managed to use the 'F'-word in almost-throwaway, pleasant, everyday dialogue, Jason's Bateman seemed to explode with X-rated expletives in every scene. Perhaps no one had used the 'C'-word more often or more convincingly on screen.

Although the troubled character of Bateman was clearly

far removed from Jason's own charming, upbeat and good-humoured personality, it wasn't hard to imagine how he had managed to dredge up such anger, bitterness and emotion for such a difficult role at this point in his personal life. Off-screen, his seven-year relationship with Kelly Brook had broken down, and his former girlfriend was now in the arms of her *Survival Island/Three* co-star Billy Zane. Jason consoled himself by starting a brief relationship with one of *London*'s minor actresses, Sophie Monk, who played the part of Lauren.

Jason's film releases from 2003 to 2005 had proved that there was much more to Jason the actor than many had imagined. Following *Lock Stock ...* and *Snatch*, he'd modestly portrayed himself in interviews as a lucky man who'd simply been in the right place at the right time. Some had accused him of simply scowling like a soap star rather than acting like a film star, and his detractors had suggested he still lacked the emotional intelligence to be a good Hollywood actor. Due to his lack of theatrical experience, many early reviews seemed to suggest that Jason's success in Guy Ritchie's films had only been because the characters of Bacon and Turkish had been specifically written for him and therefore fitted him like boxing gloves. Some critics complained that he didn't seem to *do much* onscreen except frown and look dangerous, but then the same was once written about Clint Eastwood in his now-iconic spaghetti westerns. Sergio Leone's *The Good, the Bad and the Ugly* (1966) was heavily criticised on its release for its lack of dialogue; no one, including Clint's character Blondie, spoke for the first ten and a half minutes.

But *The Italian Job*, *Cellular* and *London* had proved that Jason wasn't a one-dimensional actor with limitations. He was gradually developing his reputation as a forceful film-star talent – crucially, when he was on screen, you couldn't take your eyes off him. He had already managed to get inside the heads of some extremely diverse, difficult characters – good, bad *and* ugly. 'We're just weak on the inside like every man,' he would later observe of these more challenging roles. 'We've got a tough exterior, some are a lot tougher than others, of course. Deep down, they bleed, they feel pain, they're emotionally scarred and they struggle with that ... that makes them real and therefore you can get behind them.'

Jason had shown that he could hold his own in the company of Hollywood legends as major as Donald Sutherland while at the same time plotting the next stage in his rise towards global action hero. The *Transporter* franchise was up and running – he would be shooting *Transporter 2* in 2004 – and this would help build his growing reputation throughout the decade.

But at this point, apparently settled in America, Jason's greatest challenge as an actor was on the horizon. True to his word, he had loyally accepted the lead role in *Revolver*, an incredibly complex psychological film, written and directed by his old friend Guy Ritchie.

* * *

It would be Jason's third time around with Ritchie (his fourth if you counted Guy's executive involvement in *Mean Machine*). They knew the way one another worked – their quirks and their strengths. From Jason's point of view it offered an experience that was unlike working with any other director: 'I'd just come back from *Transporter 2* in Miami,' he recalled.

'Literally had a week off, flew back to London and started on *Revolver*. So one movie to the next, it was completely different. Guy had not changed anything from the way he directs, even the people he used. It was like an old band getting back together playing a few of the old songs.'

It may have felt like an old band but there was little doubt about the identity of *Revolver*'s lead singer. As Guy Ritchie confirmed, 'Jason was always the choice, because he and I had been playing chess and talking about this very premise – you are ultimately your own worst enemy – for many years. So it seemed like a natural fit.'

In many ways, returning to the Ritchie fold was a comfortable choice for Jason. He'd spoken warmly and often about Guy's impact on his life and there was a real sense of excitement and expectation about the reunion. It seemed that Jason was now a conquering hero, coming home to star in a potentially great British movie. Whereas Guy's last film had been the critically battered *Swept Away* (2002), Jason's reputation was rising fast as a result of *The Italian Job*, *The Transporter* and *Cellular*.

Having secured Brad Pitt, Dennis Farina and Benicio del Toro for *Snatch* in 2000, and having directed with his wife Madonna on *Swept Away*, Guy Ritchie now cast Ray Liotta, Vincent Pastore and André Benjamin alongside Jason. Pastore was well known for his mobster character Salvatore 'Big Pussy' Bonpensiero in *The Sopranos*, while Benjamin (a.k.a. André 3000) had found fame in the hip hop duo OutKast with tracks such as 'Ms Jackson' and the worldwide number one 'Hey Ya!'

Alongside Jason, Ray Liotta was the other star turn. Liotta had made his name in memorable movies such as *Something*

Wild, *Goodfellas* and *Field of Dreams*, often playing disturbingly convincing madmen. For *Revolver* he'd pull out all the psycho stops as the strangely named Dorothy Macha, a cruel casino owner convinced he was going to be shafted by his nemesis – the revenge-seeking conman and gambler Jake Green. United on screen, evil-eyed, mentally unstable and in close-up, Statham and Liotta proved to be a terrifying combination. Unsurprisingly, their formidable onscreen chemistry didn't go unnoticed and they would later be signed up to work together again on 2007's *In the Name of the King: A Dungeon Siege Tale*.

Playing Jake Green, Jason admitted that he had found himself stretched as both an actor and as an individual. The mindset of his character was completely different to the sorts of roles he was more used to. As Jason explained, 'I've always been the physical guy on the street corner, trying to exact money from people's pockets. That was an easy thing, it was A, B, C. But here I get to tell people what they think they want to hear, give them just a little of what they think they want and then entice them to give up a bit of money. It's almost like, you want what is in the right hand yet what you are really looking for is in the left hand, but the one on the right is covered in tinsel and it's far more attractive.'

Revolver was undeniably an internal, complicated film, totally different to Guy Ritchie's previous movies. It wasn't cops and robbers or black comedy or even good guys versus dark villains, it was much more challenging. The film grappled with ideas about man's battle against *himself* and his own mental failings – perhaps a difficult concept to transfer to the screen without alienating some of the viewers.

With the tag-line 'Your mind will not accept a game this

big', Ritchie says he called it *Revolver* because 'The idea is there's a voice in your head, it's the one that's revolving, it's both the one that seduces you and punishes you. I found the concept so attractive because I'm so interested in cons. Once I found out that the mind works the same way a conman works, then I was afraid the premise was too good for me to ignore.'

Shot on location in London and the Isle of Man, *Revolver* seemed to be set in a strangely anonymous metropolis of western and oriental gangsters with Italian-American and cockney accents. Some critics lazily called it a 'Vegas heist' movie but at times the locations appeared less like Nevada and more like a neon-lit gangland Manchester or Blackpool, complete with a snooker hall called Sticks & Balls.

Looking like a ravaged long-haired country-rock star (maybe a decadent lost Beach Boy or a casualty from The Byrds), Jason's Jake Green made the rough journey from ex-con revenge-seeker towards a state of enlightenment, carrying out his plan like a grandmaster chess player by obeying maxims such as 'You can only get smarter by playing a smarter opponent'.

Attempting to describe what made his character tick, Jason explained that 'he's many things. Jake's trying to use the smart way to get himself out of all the nonsense with the guns. He's trying to use his brain to do the talking, which is kind of a nice break for me 'cause I'm usually doing all the fighting and the shooting. It was nice to have to out-think the opponent instead of just beating them senseless.' But in essence, and to utilise the language of chess strategy, Jake is a conman who transforms himself from a pawn at the beginning of the film into the king by the end of it.

Working with Guy Ritchie on location, Jason found that little had changed in terms of the atmosphere, creativity and enjoyment the director brought to all his projects. The same family ethos, that Guy had cultivated for the previous two films on which they had both worked, still existed and, more than anything else, Jason simply enjoyed acting under the direction of Guy. Doing what he loved best, Jason felt able – and actively encouraged – to offer creative input and have a few laughs at the same time. As Jason said, 'Guy has got an easy way of directing. It's serious and then it's not. He gets the job done and then we have a bit of fun, too. I particularly like the experience of working with someone who can change dialogue as we go, if it doesn't sound quite right ... So it's great. We have a great understanding of working together now.'

Unlike many other directors, Guy knew exactly what he wanted and how to achieve it. And it wasn't just Jason who enjoyed the creative, positive atmosphere on set: Vincent Pastore also found Ritchie's approach to film-making refreshing. Vincent recalled that, 'He doesn't do a lot of takes. He's got the same crew that's been working with him on all his movies, and these guys know what he wants. So he tells them to set up a shot, he'll come in and say, "OK, I got ten guys sitting around a table. I want this, this, this and this." He'll walk out, play chess with Jason, come back, and they'll shoot.'

And so the chess rivalry between Statham and Ritchie continued. But for the first time, chess also played a key role in *Revolver*, on camera as well as off. The film's plot was mapped out like a lengthy chess match and Jake's life seemed to move reluctantly and unstoppably towards an end-game. He was constantly seen outwitting his opponent Avi (André

Benjamin), but gradually realised he'd simply been conned into believing he was the better player. When the crunch match came, he lost out. Checkmate. Perhaps Guy Ritchie – who had been fiercely competitive with Jason at chess, judo and jiu-jitsu since they'd first met on *Lock Stock . . .* – enjoyed picturing his good mate 'Jay' losing on the big screen.

Jason found filming *Revolver* a stimulating if challenging experience, and developed great chemistry with his two 'guardian angels', the loan sharks played by André Benjamin and Vincent Pastore – two very different actors and personalities. Jason explained that 'André's very much an individual, his fashion sense, his demeanour, his very clean sort of living style . . . he's a smooth dude and a good mate. It was great because you've got him and then you've got Vincent Pastore, on the other hand; you couldn't get two people more at opposite ends of the spectrum, and yet they're my two best friends in the film. These are the guys who are going to save me from myself.'

'Big Pussy' Pastore would return the compliments, describing Jason as 'a very talented person' and André as a smart guy who learned his lines, adding that 'a lot of the time you work with a musician and they're too busy smoking dope'.

But despite the strength of the cast, and the great sense of ambition expressed through Guy Ritchie's original ideas and vivid direction, *Revolver* was always going to struggle commercially. The initial market-research reactions were negative. Audiences and critics alike had naturally been expecting a comedic gangster-style reprise from Ritchie, Statham and the crew, perhaps with elements of *The Transporter* thrown in for good measure due to Luc Besson's involvement as the co-producer who adapted the screenplay.

Guy's complicated, ambitious film required Jason to stretch his talents far beyond his martial arts and action-hero roles, and Jason appreciated that the whole point, this time around, was to try something different: 'I don't think Guy ever made this to be *Transformers* or something a bit more commercial,' he said, somewhat defensively, while promoting *Revolver*. 'He's never going to make a movie like that. Guy does something a bit different. Even *Snatch* and *Lock Stock* . . . were never going to be front-runners to steal the weekend.'

More than *Lock Stock* . . . or *Snatch*, *Revolver* deliberately attempted to make the viewer *think*. The concepts and ideas that it tries to put across were provocative and, as Jason said, 'It deserves a fair amount of conversation. It deserves a second review, definitely. People will visit it again. I think you'll see more the next time you go and the more you can talk about it with somebody I think you'll learn a lot about yourself. I know I learned a lot about myself making this movie.'

Revolver was the Marmite of movies: you either really loved it or you *really* hated it. *Screen International*'s critic savaged it as a 'convoluted, risibly overwrought muddle', declaring that audiences would be 'bewildered and disappointed'. The *Hollywood Reporter* complained of the film's 'pretentious style and fractured storytelling', stating that 'the movie spins wildly in circles, continually doubling back on itself, repeating scenes – once even backward – and lines of dialogue until a viewer loses a grip on what is supposed to be real'. Others pointed to the briefly bizarre and confusing use of manga animation within the action, suggesting that Guy Ritchie had tried but failed to emulate Quentin Tarantino's achievements in *Kill Bill*.

Naturally, Guy Ritchie battled hard to defend his own film and his ambition to tackle something different and a bit more experimental. Ritchie conceded that 'It's not *Snatch* and if you liked *Snatch* you're not necessarily going to like *Revolver*' – while honestly admitting 'I understand how hard it is to get the movie. But I've done a couple of great romps and riots and black comedies so why not do something more challenging? Why not do something with a few more layers to it? You have to do something more interesting for yourself and I think this kind of thing should be embraced. It's all about the pursuit of knowledge about yourself. If you want to know more about yourself and what weaknesses you have then this is the only way to go about it.' Just in the same way that Jason was challenging himself to play new and diverse roles, Guy was trying to expand his repertoire, but with less success. The style of the films he had built his reputation upon, through *Lock Stock ...* and *Snatch*, proved hard to shake off.

Guy had tried to break out of the pigeon-hole that now threatened to limit the way his films were perceived, and resorted to what some might call 'managing expectations'. 'I'm trying to advertise what's written on the tin,' he claimed, in a gesture that was hardly likely to attract a wider cinema audience, 'to make sure that when you go and buy the tin, it is what it says. So don't go to this movie if you're not interested in thinking. But if you're interested in tricks of the mind, then this is the movie for you.'

Unfortunately, the critical backlash against Guy's 'tricks of the mind' would prevent *Revolver* from being widely distributed in the USA until 2007, by which time Ritchie had re-edited the film's narrative into a slightly more commercial, easier-to-grasp form that was intended to be more viewer-friendly.

The condemnation was far from unanimous, however. In Europe, *Empire* declared that 'Statham delivers the first tour de force performance of his career', while *Sight & Sound* argued that the onscreen chemistry between Jason and André Benjamin was the strongest aspect of *Revolver*, producing an 'intensity and natural animosity that's immediately believable'. More positive still, Jameson Kowalczyk of *Ion Cinema* suggested that although 'it is not complex in a David Lynch kind of way; its intent is far more direct, and unlike the fluffy pseudo philosophy of *Donnie Darko*, *Revolver* has something substantial once you've peeled back the layers. It is really quite a brilliant film, but that doesn't mean that audiences will like it.'

For various reasons, and with the benefit of hindsight, Guy Ritchie's reputation as an original writer and director seemed to suffer for several years following *Revolver*. At the UK premiere in London's Leicester Square on 20 September 2005, Ritchie and his wife Madonna were booed because they had refused to sign autographs. In contrast, Jason spent an hour signing and posing for photographs in front of the 2,000-strong crowd. Later, Guy's 2008 'sex and thugs and rock 'n' roll' feature *RocknRolla* would also struggle to make a commercial impact, but his 2009 take on *Sherlock Holmes* (starring Robert Downey Jr and Jude Law) would be seen as a welcome and stylish return to commercial form.

Jason would look back fondly on *Revolver*, even though he would regard it as 'pretty tough'. With typical loyalty towards Guy Ritchie he had refused to criticise or judge the film in comparison with either *Lock Stock . . .* or *Snatch*: 'I've got such a fond memory of *Lock Stock . . .* because it was the first movie I ever did. So I feel that it is the most charming. *Snatch* was the funniest and I had such a great experience on it. I met Brad (Pitt) and Dennis Farina and Benicio del Toro – all these Hollywood people coming to London. It was like, "Geez this is amazing!" So I have very fond memories of those two.' But when talking about *Revolver*, Jason also shared an unguarded moment of affection for Guy: '*Revolver* was such an ambitious, personal movie for Guy, and I know Guy so well that this means so much to me too. So I can't really pick and choose, they all have their own significant importance to me.'

In terms of the ongoing development of his own film career, Jason would later admit that working on *Revolver* had affected him profoundly: 'It's been really life-changing for me,' he reflected. 'Every movie you learn something new, something different about yourself, and you gain more confidence, and I don't think there's any substitute for experience. You have to live it and feel it to become a better actor. I've come all this way.'

In terms of the roles he accepted, Jason had also learned the vital importance of choosing parts that suited him at each stage of his unfolding career. If he wanted to simply be viewed as an action hero – perhaps the greatest action hero of his generation – then he would have to accept being typecast and stomach the criticism that he was a one-dimensional performer; action films rarely spared much time for intelligent dialogue or complex character development. However, if Jason really wanted to keep his options open *and* be regarded as an all-round cinematic talent who could play the leading man in any genre – like, say, Brad Pitt or Tom Cruise – then he would need to carefully select future roles to prevent Hollywood producers from pigeon-holing him.

Guy Ritchie's meteoric rise and apparent fall within a mere five years must have affected Jason. Although Guy would resurrect his commercial fortunes a few years later with *Sherlock Holmes*, Jason realised that critical failure could be extremely destructive and damaging. As he observed, 'You do a couple of bad films and you're on the scrap heap. So you have to be smart with your choices – that's the hard part!'

Thankfully, in his manager Steve Chasman and his *Transporter* mentor Luc Besson, Jason had sound advisors around him. They knew what the actor was capable of, and were determined not to let him burn out in one particular genre of film-making. Jason himself clearly had a good eye for clever scripts, strong original ideas and interesting and creative directors. He was perceptive with his choices and seemed to achieve the difficult balance between physical films and more dramatically challenging roles; even though, at the peak of his fitness in the mid-to-late 2000s, focusing on the action-hero route would have been both easy and financially lucrative.

By the middle of the first decade of the twenty-first century, Jason had plenty of options. He could try his hand at serious drama and he could also have some street-fighting, stunt-driving, action-adventure fun. Things might not have gone so well for him personally, but in professional terms he was having the time of his life.

CHAPTER EIGHT:

CRANKING IT UP

Jason Statham had begun to convince film producers and audiences he could definitely deliver as a leading man in Hollywood. Entering the second half of the 2000s he had established himself as a rising star, a box-office attraction; on his own terms in *The Transporter* and *Transporter 2*, and also as a member of an all-star ensemble in *The Italian Job*. The dark, independent movie *London* had been far better than the critical reception it received (or the box office weight it punched) and, aside from audience disappointment at the complex nature of Guy Ritchie's *Revolver*, Jason had come through both projects with a stronger reputation as a character actor. He'd even looked convincing with hair.

Each of the movies Jason had made since he moved to Hollywood in 2000 had enhanced his status in a variety of ways. Women generally – and American women in particular – seemed to like his British-tough-guy, diamond-in-the-rough appeal. In five years he'd proved he could adapt his skills to different genres such as action adventure, black comedy, science fiction, martial arts, and even art-house with *London*. His sense of humour had begun to shine through, particularly in *The Italian Job*, and he'd developed a winning smile on screen to match his menacing scowl.

Male audiences admired the way 'The Stath' handled himself, and critics – even if they sometimes undervalued his talents as a dramatic character actor – couldn't help but respect his convincing portrayal of a tough guy who could take care of himself. The man was a natural-born athlete and, clearly, a skilful martial artist.

Aside from Daniel Craig as James Bond, Britain hadn't produced a *bona fide* action-movie star before, or certainly not since Roger Moore had suavely taken on the role of 007. The stunts that Jason found himself performing and the company he was starting to keep – Brad Pitt, Charlize Theron, Tom Cruise, Kim Basinger, Donald Sutherland, and Jet Li in particular – convinced even sceptical observers that he knew what he was doing.

Significantly, rather than the jealousy that often surrounded artists who had made the big time, there seemed to be a genuine feeling – within the British press *and* in the cinema stalls – that Jason had worked hard for his fame. He had got there by sheer guts and determination, not to mention talent. Perhaps there was also an element of sympathy for him, following the break-up of his relationship with Kelly Brook in 2004. Here was a man, it seemed, who had achieved the dream and conquered Hollywood, but at a high personal price.

There was nothing phoney about Jason Statham. You got what you saw and more than you expected. He was convincing and engaging on the big screen. Nevertheless, as the history of cinema had proved, actors were only as good as their last film. Although *Revolver* hadn't worked for Guy Ritchie, Jason defended his old friend manfully, supporting Ritchie's right to be experimental and to deliver fresh ideas and original concepts. But now Jason had to deliver another successful film himself to continue his ascent through the ranks of Hollywood's leading men.

Filmed in Seattle in 2005, he starred in *Chaos*, a big-budget crime drama written and directed by Tony Giglio. With Jason billed as the lead character, above Ryan Phillippe and Wesley Snipes, *Chaos* illustrated how far he had come. Snipes had been one of the great action hero hopes of the 1990s but clearly Lionsgate, the production company – famous as home of the *Saw* franchise – viewed Jason as the bigger box-office draw.

On paper, *Chaos* seemed like a clichéd idea. Jason's character, Quentin Conners, was an experienced detective who had been suspended from duty for failing to prevent the death of a congressman's daughter during a kidnapping. However, he soon recalled to the police force when, during a major hostage crisis at a bank, the main perpetrator Lorenz (Wesley Snipes) demanded to deal only with Conners. Criticised by some of his colleagues, Conners had to work with a 'babysitter', Shane Dekker (Ryan Phillippe), to redeem his reputation.

Sold as a film about bitter and twisted policemen ('between corruption and the end of a gun lies chaos'), and with the tag-line 'A stand-off where nobody stands down', *Chaos* was tautly written and cleverly plotted. One reviewer complained of 'the film's pervading lack of authenticity', but it was full of well-worked twists and turns. Unlike *The Italian Job* or Jason's later British film *The Bank Job*, the heist in *Chaos* was carried out in a sophisticated, hi-tech 21st-century fashion, by planting a virus in the bank's computer system so as to enable the criminal mastermind to siphon off millions of dollars from internet accounts.

Despite an understated growl of an American accent – possibly inspired by one of his heroes, Clint Eastwood – Jason acted Conners with real conviction and kept his character's true motives hidden beneath the surface. It was a strong theatrical performance rather than an action role; the only motorcycle chase featured Ryan Phillippe rather than Jason. And, although Conners didn't get the girl (Detective Teddy Galloway, played by Justine Waddell), he'd clearly had a relationship with her in the past and rejected her attempts to rekindle the passion.

The moral heart of the film rested on whether or not Quentin Conners was a good cop seeking redemption or a bad cop bent on revenge. Jason's achievement was to create a troubled-yet-likeable lead character and leave the audience guessing until the last ten minutes. Perhaps *Chaos*' only real weakness lay in the old-fashioned Agatha Christie-style ending in which, aided by flashbacks, Jason and Ryan Phillippe had a lengthy phone conversation explaining the 'chaos theory' behind the heist, revisiting the more complex elements in the previous ninety minutes of drama, and tidying up the loose ends.

Despite this, Jason, Ryan Phillippe and Wesley Snipes all received critical praise for their 'impressive performances' (*Reel Films*) in *Chaos*. In total contrast, Jason would also be mentioned in despatches for his brief but strange comedic cameo as the over-the-top French football coach Yves Gluant in *The Pink Panther* (2006) alongside Steve

Martin, Kevin Kline, Beyoncé Knowles and Jean Reno.

Given the wide variety of roles he'd already played in the USA, it was hard to guess what film genre Jason would attempt next. Martial arts or melodrama? Comedy or crime? Action or art-house? The answer, in the form of *Crank*, exceeded even the wildest speculation.

You could say what you wanted about Guy Ritchie – most critics often did – but you couldn't argue with the original and visionary way he had directed both *Lock Stock . . .* and *Snatch*. For all its problems, and despite the backlash against its complex psychological plot, *Revolver* remained an intriguingly different if difficult type of British movie. Yes, it was easy to see Tarantino's influence but, compared with a lot of films made in the UK in the early 21st century, that wasn't neces- sarily a bad thing. Whatever views critics passed on Ritchie and *Revolver*, clearly he had inspired a generation of young film- makers to look at cinema genres in a radically different way.

Without Ritchie or Tarantino, Brian Taylor and Mark Nev- eldine might not have had the courage to create something as heart-stoppingly fast-paced, as mad-caply brutal, as visually weird and cartoonishly violent, or even as unpleasantly funny as 2006's *Crank*. Set in a futuristic/nihilistic Los Angeles, where life would be decadent, brutish and short, it was like a drugged-up new-wave punk-rock picture riddled with fast cuts, freeze frames, screen-saving graphics and crash zooms.

With its sales pitch of 'poison in his veins, vengeance in his heart', Jason's character Chev Chelios was truly living on borrowed time. The trailer in itself was a work of art; fast- cut to Motörhead's 'Ace of Spades', it was a burning-rubber, car-chasing,　sex-and-drugs-and-guns-and-*more*-drugs-and- rock-'n'-roll showcase for a strong but simple idea that deliberately spoiled the film's climax in the opening voice-over: 'My name is Chev Chelios ... and today is the day I die.'

From the opening scenes of the film, when Chev realises he has been lethally injected with a 'Beijing cocktail', we know we are in for a wild ride. Once his 'Dr Feelgood', played by country star Dwight Yoakam, has revealed that the only way he can survive the poison is by keeping his adrenaline constantly high, Chev has to do everything and *anything* he can think of to keep up his energy levels.

It was a clever plot with a ticking clock. Could Chev find an antidote and exact hideous revenge on the gangsters who were behind his death sentence? And, if he was going to achieve this, then how the hell would the film-makers square the outcome with the audience's prior knowledge that our mad, bad and dangerous-to-know anti-hero would inevitably die at the journey's end?

'Another interesting character, slightly different from what I've done before,' said Jason, trying to analyse the utterly inexplicable Chev. 'He's much more of a less internal guy, more of a desperate man doing desperate things, trying to stay alive.'

In one classic scene, when he was on the verge of passing out as the poison coursed through his veins, Chev manically raided a petrol station and stocked up with energy drinks like Red Bull, Monster and energy-boost bars. Other life-saving emergency sources of adrenaline included fits of extreme violence, gun crimes, mad driving stunts, and use of hard drugs (taking coke from the floor of a scuzzy club toilet or inhaling nasal sprays laced with ephedrine), plus sex in very public places with his wonderfully scatty girlfriend Eve, played by Amy Smart. 'I love Amy,' Jason once said in a brotherly way, 'She's a classy, beautiful woman.'

Smart had made a name for herself in the TV series *Scrubs* and in the feature film rom-com *Just Friends* (with Ryan Reynolds), and had recently worked on *Unhitched* with Seth Green (one of Jason's co-stars in *The Italian Job*).

Unlike Frank Martin in *The Transporter*, Quentin Conners in *Chaos* or Jake Green in *Revolver*, Chev Chelios had few redeeming features; a mercenary assassin who was little better than the evil bastards he was constantly trying to eliminate, chiefly the bald, tattooed Latino gangster Ricky Verona (Jose Pablo Cantillo) and the crazed, smiling mafia boss Carlito (Carlos Sanz). At least, facing imminent death, Chev was honest with Eve about his unorthodox day job and the mistakes he had made in life. But, as she observed early in the film, rather than the movie-star pin-up and heart-throb she had hoped for, he had the look of a serious crack addict with a terrible wardrobe and personal hygiene problems.

Brian Taylor and Mark Neveldine stopped at nothing to guarantee mad, colourful action in every frame. Perhaps the comic-book violence in *Crank* owed more to Tarantino than Guy Ritchie – brutal, black-comedic horror images of severed hands holding revolvers, fingers being shot off, a gangster repeatedly punctured with needles under a sweatshop factory sewing machine, heads exploding with blood and brains ...

In true Ritchie style, however, the slow-motion, split screen and rapid editing were accompanied by a fantastically appropriate and angry soundtrack featuring titles such as 'Mental Health' by Quiet Riot, 'New Noise' by Refused, 'Bandera' by Control Machete, plus assorted contributions from an outfit called the Black Mob Group. There was also a surreal sequence in which Jason, wearing a hospital gown barely covering his manhood, performed unlikely stunts on a stolen police motorcycle, to the sound of Harry Nilsson's version of 'Everybody's Talkin''.

Crank was a very funny, often crude, violent, action-packed and strangely sexy film that gave Jason the opportunity to prove he had a real sense of humour. Those who didn't like the film either took it too seriously or judged it in terms of political correctness. Yes, it could have been interpreted as the story of a white Anglo-Saxon in conflict with various ethnic elements of the criminal underworld. And yes, the only women portrayed in the picture seemed to be either 'eye-candy' offering sexual favours, or slightly screwball, like Eve. But it was like an extreme version of a Guy Ritchie film in the sense that the audience was forced to take sides with a villain in conflict with even worse villains. There was no simplistic, palatable battle between good and evil.

'*Crank* is just like from the fucking stratosphere,' observed Jason. 'It's so out there, so wacky, so unbelievable, but at the same time it's that Neveldine and Taylor edgy, mad film-making. It's fun, it's entertainment. Some people think it's sheer horseshit but every person I've met has actually said it's terrific. I'm sure there're some people that don't like it. You can't please everybody but there's a lot of people that love it and I, particularly, love it.'

His co-star and *Crank* girlfriend Amy Smart echoed Jason's views on the film and also offered personal insights into working with him: 'He's a great badass on screen, but he's definitely very humble. He can be shy at times. I think it helps that we were both being so completely outrageous together. It's kind of like a rollercoaster, when you're climbing up the tracks and you anticipate, "Oh my god – I am just going to have to surrender to this crazy ride!" It has that adrenaline-rush feeling because you're putting everything on the line and you hope that it turns out OK.'

Arguably the most difficult scene they filmed together involved Eve's attempts to save Chev's life by getting his 'mojo' working and his adrenaline flowing in the middle of LA's Chinatown. With crowds looking on, Jason had to simulate sex with Amy. 'Trying to do an aggressive sex scene is quite difficult,' he laughed, 'especially in a public place with a crowd of screaming extras with their little camera phones going click-click, taking pictures of your pasty white ass. I've had my fair share of bedroom antics in films, but they were a little more private.'

In the spirit of *Crank*, Amy really enjoyed the ride: 'It's just another way to live out a fantasy because you wouldn't probably do this in real life. It's completely over the top and funny at the same time – because it doesn't take itself too seriously. Half the takes are just messed up because we just start laughing. But I'm pretty game – I'm not scared to look like a complete fool in front of people. It's just not one of my insecurities.'

Most of the positive reviews focused on the film's incredible pace and punch. The 'lad mags' loved it and so did the tabloids: 'a non-stop adrenaline thrill ride,' screamed the *Daily Mirror*. *Empire* called it 'a hardcore action classic'; for *Total Film* it was 'a great little adrenaline rush of a B-movie'; while the *New York Times* observed 'the movie has been likened to *Speed* but in this case Statham is the bus'.

Even the film critic Charles Gant, in picking his *Sight & Sound* 'Films of the Year' for 2006, apologetically embraced the madness by placing *Crank* up there alongside *United 93* and *This is England*: 'Yes, the dumbass, entirely reprehensible film starring Jason Statham. Never mind Statham's generic performance, the absurd misogyny and the non-stop homophobic insults, *Crank* won my affection for its try-anything originality. First-time film-makers Mark Neveldine and Brian Taylor showcased a directorial style that was utterly unfettered, presumably because nobody told them about the rules. My only quibble is that, because of its relentless pacing, the eighty-seven minutes feels much longer: it's like you've just lived through a war.'

Having been made on a relatively small budget, *Crank* generated $45million at the box office and became a cult film. Aside from providing Jason with another unforgettable action man role, it also created a great working relationship with writers/directors Taylor and Neveldine. Significantly, in the *New York Times*, Taylor praised Jason's all-round abilities and courage in contrast with his Hollywood rivals, stating 'we have a generation of young American actors who are good but soft'.

However, despite the great anti-social anti-hero appeal of their central character Chev Chelios, Taylor and Neveldine would have one major problem going forward with their *Crank* franchise. In the final frames of the film, Chev Chelios had clearly been killed in a 3,000-foot fall from a helicopter and was last seen lying in an LA street like road-kill, blood pouring from his mouth, unblinking pupils madly dilated; the eyes of a dead man.

Even Jason believed there would not – and *could not* – be a sequel. But then ...

'They [Neveldine and Taylor] said to me, "You know we've written *Crank 2*." And I said, "There's no way!" and they literally sent it over. They write very quickly and they sent me the script and I was thumbing through it with a box of tissues, just laughing and crying, going, "This is absolutely silly! When do we make it!" They come in with a big shovel, that's the fucking start of the next film, right there, bang, on the street.'

Unsurprisingly, the brilliant hook-line in the *Crank 2: High Voltage* publicity proclaimed, almost religiously, 'He Was Dead ... But He Got Better', and 'You Can't Keep A Dead Man Down!'

Rather than beginning with salvation and redemption, *Crank 2* found Chev Chelios (Jason) in the hands of Chinese mobsters and evil surgeons who wanted to steal his apparently indestructible vital organs. After escaping from their clutches – they had removed his heart and were eyeing up his meat and two veg! – Chev realised they were planning to transplant his heart into the failing body of a lecherous old triad boss called Poon Dong, played by David Carradine. (Carradine had memorably played the great philosophical martial artist Kane in the 1970s TV series *Kung Fu*, and also starred in the original *Death Race 2000*.)

As Chev Chelios raced around Los Angeles, desperately searching for his 'strawberry tart', he was being kept alive by a temporary battery-powered heart. But whereas pure adrenaline had kept him going in the first *Crank* film, this time he needed massive jolts of electricity to hot-wire his major organ. Failing that, skin-on-skin friction with another human being helped do the trick, leading to Chev's various close encounters with his pole-dancing ex-girlfriend Eve (Amy Smart), a mad prostitute called Ria (Bai Ling) and even an old lady on a Zimmer frame at the race-track.

Crank had received an '18' certificate for 'strong violence, language and drug use'; *Crank 2*'s 'R'-rating was due to 'frequent strong violence, gore, sex and very strong language'. But alongside the more hardcore material there was also plenty of humour as Jason's character charged his battery-heart with jump leads from a passing car, or borrowed the electric shock pads from a crash team in hospital, or plugged himself into the mains, ignoring those 'Danger of Death' warning signs.

Plus, there were some weird flashbacks – one featuring 'Ginger' Spice Girl Geri Halliwell as the troublesome young Chev's mum – and a very odd fighting puppets sequence in which Chev took on the Chinese gangster Johnny Wang in scenes reminiscent of the battling Cold War presidents in Frankie Goes to Hollywood's 'Two Tribes' video.

For better or worse – *Nuts* magazine gave it four out of five stars and *Zoo*'s review read simply 'awesome' – *Crank 2* was even more sexually charged than the first film. As Amy Smart explained, 'because of the scene in Chinatown in the original film, Eve became very sexually liberated and decided to pursue pole-dancing as a way of continuing that exploration. I took a number of pole-dancing classes to get ready for the scene in *Crank 2: High Voltage*. Jason's character now has an artificial heart. He has to create friction with his body to keep his heart working. The directors found many more outrageous things he could do to keep his heart rate up. Friction is the key word in this one – friction as in he needs to rub up against something to cause friction in his body. And yes, I definitely put two and two together and assist him in that.'

You only needed to watch the hilarious high-friction scenes between Chev (Jason) and Eve (Amy), screwing in the middle of a race-track with horses thundering past them and over them, to get a measure of the picture, although as she pointed out, the action was actually a lot less fun than it looked: 'There is a part in the film where I'm getting sprayed with a fire hose down a horse race-track. It's just one of those massive water hoses that can literally spray you, like, thirty feet. That just felt so disgusting – being in the mud and there's horseshit in the mud – and it just felt dirty and gross. I needed a shower after.'

But Jason wasn't complaining about his new role as an onscreen Casanova. Throughout his early film career it always seemed as if directors had deliberately cut away as soon as he stripped off and got involved in love action. His few edited moments of conquest, in *The Transporter* (rated '15') and *The Italian Job* (rated '12'), barely made the finished films, while in *London* his anger and bitterness was fuelled by rejection and impotence. As he'd once joked, 'Every time they write in a romantic part for me, there'd always be this inability for me to get it on with the women. To be honest, that's getting rather frustrating.'

Suddenly – having been filmed in *Crank*, bare-arsed in Chinatown, shagging Eve, and also receiving an in-car blow-job from her during a high-speed police chase – in *Crank 2: High Voltage* Jason's Chev was seen playing the porn star in the middle of LA's race-track. He had gone from one extreme to the other.

Nevertheless, he was unapologetically pleased with both films, fully realising that they'd broken new ground, created another franchise he could build on, and gathered a considerable cult following. When *Crank 2* came out he said, 'I'm very proud of what I did in *Crank* ... it's an action comedy and it's meant for the kind of audience that likes this sort of thing. If you saw the first film and you were into it then you're going to love this one.'

He was right. Although he wisely, self-deprecatingly noted that 'you ain't ever gonna get an Academy Award for doing *Crank* and you certainly won't for doing all the other movies I've done', many reviewers reacted in a surprisingly positive way, noting how the film perfectly honed in on its late-night, young-male, escapist-slacker target audience. One American film website described it as 'a terrific sleazoid treat ... unabashedly shameless and willing to try anything for the sake of a jolt, *Crank 2: High Voltage* is like a convenience store corn dog. It's undeniably bad for you but satisfies like little else.'

The best, appropriately tongue-in-cheek, review came from Bill Gibron: 'This is cinema as sugar rush, a non-stop barrage of references, homages and inventions that add up to fuel-injected fun for the newly pubescent crowd. Adults will be shocked by the language and violence, while women will be protesting the ample nudity and slight misogyny. But if you're fourteen to eighteen, hopped up on hormones, fresh off your daily dose of Ritalin and ready to have your short attention span verbally and visually assaulted, you'll be in for a toxic trip.'

So far, Jason hadn't made many poor choices in terms of scripts, directors or casting during the early years of his career, but one movie shot around this time tested the loyalty of even his youngest and most ardent fans. He had already had a brief, extremely successful, excursion into the video game voice-over market by playing Shrike in *Red Faction 2* and Sgt Waters in the massive-selling *Call of Duty*. *Red Faction 2*, released in 2002, featured Jason's line, 'It's like trying to find a needle in a stack of bodies', while in *Call of Duty*

(2003) he could be heard growling, 'Are you blind and deaf or just stupid?'

In the Name of the King: A Dungeon Siege Tale, directed by Uwe Boll, was a feature-length fantasy adventure based on a video game, in which Jason's character Farmer Daimon made the journey from simple peasant to heroic prince. Filmed in Vancouver in 2004, it looked like a low-rent CGI version of *Lord of the Rings* even though it also starred Jason's arch-enemy from *Revolver*, Ray Liotta, as the wicked wizard Gallian.

Of all Jason's work, *In the Name of the King* would come to be regarded as his only major failure, flopping badly in cinemas and struggling to even find an audience on DVD. Made on a lavish budget of more than $60million, it would generate a disappointing $11million in return. Unfairly, Uwe Boll would blame the film's stars for failing to help publicise the movie, even though Jason and Ray Liotta were both on location at the time of its release.

Even before the critics had started pulling Boll's film apart, Jason had already distanced himself from the project, suggesting that he had unwisely made his choice based on the presence of a martial arts choreographer rather than the strength of the script. 'I was in a completely different spot back then,' he'd recall. 'It's a kids' thing. You know, it's *for* the kids and I wanted to work with Tony Chang who is one of the most predominant action choreographers in the world. If you've ever seen *House of Flying Daggers* or *Hero*, you only have to look no further than that, an opportunity to work with someone like that stands for itself. Things change, time changes, you do things for different reasons at different periods in your life and that was back then.'

As per usual, Jason's performance would be one of the film's few saving graces. 'Statham is fine, if a bit too English bulldoggish for a farmer,' remarked one reviewer. But, generally, the overall critical response was extremely negative, such as 'If you're looking for another lame copy of every crappy sword-and-sorcery epic ever made, *In the Name of the King* is it ... This is one trip to Middle Earth that no fellowship, no matter how enchanted, could survive.'

By the time *In the Name of the King* finally reached cinema screens in the UK and USA in 2008, Jason's reputation would still be thriving due to the *Transporter* and *Crank* brands. More importantly, he had also been working on a triumvirate of diverse films – due for release in 2007 and 2008 – that would more than offset any minor video-game-inspired setbacks.

Although Jason would be critical of his second martial arts adventure with Jet Li – 'I'm very fussy, I'm very hard to please,' he told the *LA Times* – *War* (a.k.a. *Rogue*), was another Lionsgate production that proved he could share top billing with the best in the action-adventure genre.

As the trailer explained, in one of those horror-filled grizzly-bear beer-commercial deep voices that Hollywood loves so much, 'In a dark underworld ruled by fear ... a truce has protected their way of life ... until a lone assassin ... started a war ... Now, a renegade FBI agent will stop at nothing ... to get revenge ... Jason Statham and Jet Li ... are at War.'

War was a grim, misanthropic American-Oriental tale of gangland executions, car chases, gunfights and street shoot-outs in which Jason's character, FBI agent John Crawford, sought revenge on the assassin – Rogue, played by Jet Li – who had slain his Fed agency colleague and his family.

The film worked, but only up to a point. As Jason explained, the personal effect of the tragedy on Crawford's character was one of the film's great strengths, and this offered him a role he could really get his teeth into: 'You can sometimes wear the guilt of something else that is not necessarily your fault. You end up taking all the guilt and putting it on your own shoulders to the detriment of your own life and your own sanity. He points a finger at this guy Rogue and he will not stop at anything until he catches this man. Crawford thinks that if he can catch this man then all his problems will be gone ... it's like having one of your own family members killed. You want to get the man who pulled the trigger. That's what fuels Crawford's journey throughout this movie.'

Although the film was largely a two-hander, with Jason's good guy hunting down Jet Li's inscrutable villain, in dramatic terms *Rogue* worked better than their previous bigger-budget sci-fi-meets-martial-arts project together. This was perhaps because, as Jason admitted, he'd been 'in awe' of Jet during the making of *The One*.

Despite the involvement of Corey Yuen as both Martial Arts Choreographer and Second Unit Director – it would be the fourth of Corey's six films with Jason from *The One* (2001) through to *The Expendables* (2010) – some questioned the direction of Philip Atwell, who'd stepped up from making promo videos for Eminem, Dr Dre and 50 Cent. In the harsh view of the *LA Times*, Atwell seemed 'more interested in his lens fetish for sports cars and breasts than storytelling'. But, they added, 'Statham keeps it interesting with his raspy intensity'.

Before the box-office receipts were counted, and the film had failed to capture the public imagination, there'd even been talk of further screen encounters between Jason and Jet Li. 'If the movie's good – and I'm sure it will be – and people want to see another one, why not?' replied Jason. Unfortunately, *War* failed to repeat the business done by *The One*, which, on a $49-million budget, had made $72.6 million at the box office. *War*, in contrast, cost $25 million but recouped only $39 million. It had been a clever idea *and* a profitable film but it failed to find a wider audience. In truth, it simply hadn't been strong enough to generate yet another Statham franchise to match *Transporter* and *Crank*.

With honest hindsight, when he and Jet Li were filming on *The Expendables* in 2009, Jason would be openly critical of both *The One* and *War*. 'Actually, all of the movies I've done with Jet apart from this one have been no good,' he laughed. 'The first movie I did with Jet wasn't what it was supposed to have been originally ... But we enjoy working together. Both our previous films together had a kind of science fiction basis ... whereas this one [*The Expendables*] harks back to the old-school action movies that I'm more interested in doing.'

Jason was again determined to break out of the action-adventure pigeon-hole and confound attempts to label him as a mere action hero. *War* would be followed, in early 2008, by the UK release of a distinctly old-school *non-action* film, *The Bank Job* (no relation to *The Italian Job*) that offered Jason the chance to shine with a strong dramatic performance written by the creators of *The Likely Lads*, Dick Clement and Ian La Frenais.

Several years earlier Jason had been passed a script by his old friend Jason Flemyng, another of Guy Ritchie's *Lock Stock ...* and *Snatch* crew, who had also appeared in *Mean*

Machine and *Transporter 2*. Originally titled *Baker Street* but focusing on a struggling used-car dealer called Terry Leather, the comic heist plot apparently drew inspiration from an audacious and historic Lloyds Bank safety-deposit-box robbery in west London in 1971.

As Jason recalled, 'I read it and said "Yeah it's really good". Just chit-chatting among friends ... I *really* wanted to play it, that was years ago. I said, "Yeah I could do a really good job with this. Terry Leather, I think I could nail it."'

There then followed a long delay during which the producers struggled to get financial backing and Jason took on other commitments. 'I was disappointed because it was quite an entertaining ride.' By 2006, however, new life had been breathed into the project after producer Charles Roven had sent the script to director Roger Donaldson. Together they had worked on 1990's *Cadillac Man* and Roven believed that Australian-born Donaldson would be the ideal man to make the film work. 'He's done thrillers like *No Way Out*, character pieces like *The World's Fastest Indian* and action movies like *The Recruit*,' said Roven, 'and this is the kind of movie that allows you to blend all those techniques.'

Soon Steve Chasman also got involved and set up a meeting between Statham and Donaldson. 'We just clicked, he was excited, I was excited,' recalled Jason. 'I'd seen all of Roger's movies so I thought "Fuck, if he wants to work with me then I've hit the jackpot!" Next thing you know, we've got the money together and bang, off to London. Roger's probably one of the most easy-going people you will ever get to meet. And the fact he has made a bucketful of brilliant films gives us the ease to come on set and take direction without even questioning him because he's such a great film-maker. He understands different characters, the storytelling aspect and the look. He's just one of the greatest directors I have ever had to work with. I feel very lucky on that side of things.'

Although Jason was delighted that the financial backing had been found for the project, he felt it was significant – in terms of his decision to quit the British film industry and move to Hollywood – that the funding had come from overseas. 'The ironic part about making this English film,' he noted, while promoting the project abroad, 'is the fact that it's all been money raised outside the UK. It's a bit of a bugger that we can't make stories like this back home.'

Given that the writers and creators Dick Clement and Ian La Frenais had penned some of British television's greatest comedy series – not just *The Likely Lads*, but also *Porridge* and *Auf Wiedersehen, Pet* – it wasn't surprising that the original script was 1970s-style-funny rather than hard-edged realism.

'I like that this is an old-fashioned robbery,' said La Frenais. 'Instead of people breaking in using computers to hack into security systems, there are picks and shovels, digging underground, blasting through the bank and tearing those boxes apart with crowbars.'

With Roger Donaldson on board as director, *Baker Street* was renamed *The Bank Job* – possibly to cash in on the great success of Jason's role in *The Italian Job* – and became a very different proposition: 'Once Roger started doing all his research, finding all these facts and the scandal side, it just took a complete turn and became this thriller,' said Jason.

'I love the research,' said Donaldson, 'that's one of the things I really do embroil myself in. I finished up going to the newspapers of the time, to the national archives, digging up facts that have not seen the light of day since they happened in 1971.'

The scandal still sounded shocking twenty-five years on. The boxes in the vaults at Lloyds Bank, Baker Street, were believed to contain proceeds from underworld crime, involving prostitution, extortion, drugs and police corruption. The film plot suggests the robbers were allegedly recruited indirectly by British government security officials, desperate to get their hands on the contents of one particular safety deposit box. In the film this was alleged to contain incriminating photographs of high-profile public figures – notorious London gangster John Bindon and a key member of the Royal family, the Queen's sister Princess Margaret. But that remains highly speculative to say the least.

Before *The Bank Job* was even released, the *Daily Mail* ran a story about the film's revelations: 'This week, a British film, unveiled at Cannes Film Festival, provoked new suggestions that sexually-incriminating pictures were secretly taken of her in Mustique. The film suggests compromising photographs of the Princess taken on the island were at the centre of a bank robbery in London in the early Seventies. It claims that the £500,000 raid – £5million in today's money, more than the haul in The Great Train Robbery – on Lloyds Bank in Baker Street was aimed at securing the pictures.'

The *Mail*'s reporter Wendy Leigh also interviewed the model Vicki Hodge, a long-term partner of John Bindon (who died in 1993). She confirmed that Bindon had indeed had an affair with Princess Margaret and added 'it could well have been that Margaret and John's one dangerous moment was on the beach and that someone could have snatched a picture'.

Although, at the time, Bindon had apparently swapped his life of crime to play tough guys in films such as *Poor Cow*, *Performance*, *Get Carter and Barry Lyndon* – coincidentally, he was also the inspiration for Vinnie Jones' character in *Lock Stock & Two Smoking Barrels* – he would eventually stand trial for the murder of gangster Johnny Darke in 1979.

In the film the photographs had fallen into the hands of Michael X, a Trinidadian-born conman and gangster who ran the Black Panther Movement in London. Facing drug-running charges, Michael X had allegedly blackmailed the British government by threatening to publish the photographs if he was prosecuted. It was thought that Michael X had locked away the photos in a safety deposit box in Baker Street.

The original crime was branded the 'Walkie-Talkie Bank Job' because an amateur radio 'ham', Robert Rowlands, had overheard gang members talking on short-wave walkie-talkies. Rowlands alerted Scotland Yard that there was a robbery in progress somewhere within a ten-mile radius. Before MI5 could intervene, the police checked 750 banks in central London but failed to apprehend the villains. It was only on the Monday morning, when the Baker Street branch of Lloyds opened up its vaults for business, that the full extent of the crime was discovered.

As Jason's manager and *Bank Job* producer Steve Chasman commented, 'Often when I'm in London and I'm in a taxi or speaking to someone who was around at the time, they remember the Walkie-Talkie robbery and what happened. They all knew someone who knew someone who knew someone who was involved.'

So, having started out as an innocent heist caper, Jason's

latest film would now be dramatic, politically sensitive and controversial.

In stark contrast to his high-octane exploits in the slick, surreal, modern and futuristic worlds of *The Transporter*, *Crank* and *War*, Jason's character Terry Leather was a simple, struggling South London family man, in debt to violent loan sharks, who became the reluctant leader of a peaceful bunch of small-time crooks hoping to get rich quick.

'This, thankfully, hasn't been one that's tested me too much in the stunt department,' he said. 'I've replaced holding a gun with holding a pint of ale. I'm not hanging out of helicopters and doing a lot of the silliness I've been paid to do in the past. This is more of a sophisticated thriller. I'm sure it's going to be a great crowd-pleaser.'

In *The Bank Job* one of Terry's old flames, Martine (played by Saffron Burrows) gave him the tip-off about cash held in safety deposit boxes at the Baker Street branch of Lloyds. Initially unaware that Martine was having an affair with a senior figure in MI5 – who had instigated the robbery – Terry and his unprofessional gang were soon involved in a complex plot that involved underworld gangsters, porn bosses, corrupt policemen, Parliament, the Black Panthers and the Crown.

'He's talked into it by an ex-girlfriend only to find out that it involves the Royal Family, blackmail and MI5,' Jason told *Reuters*. 'It all gets very murky. I get to play a father and a husband for a change, and while it's a thriller, there's also a lot more emphasis on character and drama and intrigue than in my usual films. There's a lot going on under the surface.'

Under the surface *and* under the ground, as Terry's gang

tunnelled beneath a shoe shop and a takeaway, then into the vaults of the Baker Street bank.

Although Jason's character was far removed from the self-defensively violent action men – loners, cops, assassins, FBI agents – he had become accustomed to playing, the film was still set in a hedonistic, debauched world with violence, sexual exploitation, greed and corruption at its heart. Only four men were ever convicted of the crime and, of the property the police did manage to recover, most of it was never re-claimed. Many of the safe-deposit-box owners never came forward, fearing police prosecution if they revealed the ill-gotten contents. 'The names of many people in the film have been changed to protect the guilty,' announced the closing credits.

Roger Donaldson's film began among the swinging jet set on sun-soaked Caribbean beaches, depicting a scandalous soft-focus sexual liaison being secretly photographed. Suggesting intrigue and blackmail, these priceless photographs triggered a high-tension plot involving a series of connected murders and thefts in the far less luxurious, less fashionable, nicotine-stained environment of 1970s London.

Switching from Mustique to the sounds of Marc Bolan's T.Rex, *The Bank Job* propelled audiences into the second-hand-car world of Terry Leather Motors. But if it deliberately had the look and feel of period British TV classics such as *The Sweeney* and *Minder*, Jason was clearly determined to make sure that it didn't attract too many comparisons with his early work, or fall into obvious traps in terms of London language.

'A lot of the dialogue, we tried to stay away from, you know, with rhyming slang and all the East End stuff. We didn't want to make it sound too English. It can start falling back along the lines of Guy Ritchie stuff if you give it too much of a peppering with that kind of dialogue. It was an easy part for me to play, you know, car dealer . . . it wasn't a big stretch. It's a world that I know, wheeling and dealing cars, people that you know.'

He was being modest, as usual. Reviewers praised Jason's performance as the most convincingly dramatic of his career so far; they raved again about his 'menacing screen presence' but also complimented him on his ability to convey both the physical and emotional complexities of Terry Leather's character.

One strong feature of the film lay in the way Terry was torn between his simmering passion for old love Martine and his new, safe and secure, family life with Wendy and their kids. In the light of Jason's earlier, pre-*Crank* complaints that, frustratingly, his characters never seemed to achieve sexual satisfaction on-screen, it was a source of much amusement to critics that the scenes depicting his on-the-job action with Saffron Burrows in *The Bank Job* were not included in the film's final edit. 'I don't mind. I still got to do it,' Jason told the *Sydney Morning Herald*, revealing that he had been 'stark bollock naked' on set. 'We had to tie a few things around it to keep it in its right place,' he joked. On the same promotional trip, when asked by Australian TV host Rove McManus why the scene had been cut, Jason replied, 'My arse was far too hairy.' McManus followed this with, 'Do you keep it as a nice 12 o'clock shadow like your face?' 'Nicely groomed, yeah!' laughed Jason.

More seriously, as one of the producers, Charles Roven, observed, 'The part of Terry shows off Jason's great range as an actor. It allows him to do it all, from being the tough guy to struggling with romantic conflict. He's also incredibly likeable. He has such a great persona on screen that the audience automatically gravitates to him.'

Those hard-core Statham fans, desperate to see their action man in full fighting mode, had to be content with *The Bank Job*'s very brief, non-martial-arts punch-up near the end.

'It's hard,' Jason joked, 'because every time I do a non-fighting movie, they always write a fighting scene in . . . Two weeks into the movie, "Yeah we've got this scene, and just hit him". I think *The Bank Job* always had a moment of violence near the end. I think people want to see this guy get kicked on the floor and bashed. Our best mate gets killed, and he's responsible for that, and I think it's a good pay-off. Although I wanted to do a movie without throwing a fist or a kick or anything, I think it sort of warrants happening at this particular time, although I'm still looking for that complete romantic comedy where I don't hit anybody. One day.'

With or without Jason's privates on parade, or his ass-kicking martial arts, *The Bank Job* was number one at the UK box office on its release in 2008, no mean achievement during the same year that *Slumdog Millionaire*, *Quantum of Solace* and the remake of *Brideshead Revisited* were also filling cinemas. The film wouldn't have the same impact in America, but its star had already been signed up by one of Hollywood's biggest studios. In 2009 and 2010, he would become one of the most successful film stars on the planet.

CHAPTER NINE:

CARS AND GIRLS

In 2008, the New York film critic Armond White praised the *Transporter* movies and declared that Jason Statham had 'the best track record of any contemporary movie star'. It was a bold claim, particularly in light of the fierce box-office competition from the likes of George Clooney, Johnny Depp, Leonardo DiCaprio and Brad Pitt, but in terms of career choices and his apparently unstopp-able rise to Hollywood's A-list, few major studios would argue with it.

At the time White made his judgement, Jason had appeared in twenty films since his debut in 1998. Of these movies, arguably only two, Guy Ritchie's *Revolver* and Uwe Boll's *In the Name of the King*, had failed to deliver on their budget expectations at the box office. By conservative estimates, the remaining eighteen had grossed over *one billion* US dollars. You didn't have to be a top accountant or cash-counting film producer to recognise that Statham had become a high-class, bankable international star, one of Britain's most successful exports to Hollywood, earning well in excess of a million dollars per film while generating much, much more in profits for the studios.

In American terms, most of Jason's films had been made on a comparatively small budget. The exception had been 2003's *The Italian Job*, which had cost $60million but earned almost $180million. In contrast, *The Bank Job* had only cost $20million. Although it had been a critical and commercial hit in Europe, it came to be regarded as too British, too retrospective for American audiences and, as a result, failed to attract the box-office income expected (only $30million worldwide) – despite its qualities.

By this point, Jason had already taken the next major step in his ten-year career and was increasingly in demand among the top Hollywood studios. Life again became dominated by his hectic filming schedule and, although he was seeing LA girl-about-town Alex Zosman at the time, clearly he was far from ready to settle down with her. In fact, in one interview (in August 2008), he spoke in the future tense of his dreams of marriage and children, indicating that he was still looking for his ideal partner. 'Beggars can't be choosers,' he laughed. 'She'd need to have a sense of humour to go out with a guy like me. I would love kids. I've just got to find the right lady. I'm an old softie, me. I send flowers when they need to be sent and stuff like that. I'm thoughtful and sweet. I'm not as cold as you think I am.'

Interestingly enough, a few months later, Jason's ex-girlfriend Kelly Brook would tell the *Observer* that she regarded it as an 'achievement that I've got to thirty without having kids or getting married', stating 'I'd like to have children; marriage I have a bit of an issue with'.

For Jason, serious romance would have to wait. As he noted while completing *The Bank Job* in 2007, 'I've got enough on my plate. I've got to get ready to do two films in the next five months! It's back to fast cars and fast women, but I'm having a lot of fun doing it.' At the time, he meant *Transporter 3*, which would also be released in 2008, but following his successful series of films for Lionsgate, Jason had increasingly begun to attract the attention of the older major studios such as Warner Brothers, Paramount and, particularly, Universal Pictures.

With remakes and superheroes all the rage in Hollywood – *Indiana Jones*, *Rocky*, *Iron Man*, *Spider-Man* and so on – Universal had already committed to reworking the 1975 cult classic *Death Race 2000*. Directed by Paul Bartel and produced by Roger Corman, the original film had starred David Carradine as the driver Frankenstein and Sylvester Stallone as his bad-boy rival Machine Gun Joe. The ultimate movie for boy-racers, it had caused controversy in both Britain and the USA because of its tag-line: 'In the year 2000, hit-and-run driving is no longer a felony. It's the national sport!'

In terms of casting – forever chasing that elusive youthful, action-adventure audience – Universal looked no further than the man with the best recent record in the genre. Following a string of successes, Jason could now command larger fees and was being asked to star in bigger-budget movies. The *LA Times* guessed that the film would cost $100million to make and noted that, in casting Jason, '*Death Race* marks the first time that the thirty-four-year-old will have a major studio and blockbuster budget at his back when he jumps off a building.'

As Jason noted ahead of filming, 'Death Race is my first studio picture which has a substantially bigger budget than the other films I've done ... let's hope that continues. This is a big leap ... this is my first step into the big world of fully equipped action movies, if you will ... I'm very, very excited.'

But it wasn't just the big budget and special effects that appealed to him. The script was slick and the story was laden with excitement and thrills. It was a perfect fit for Jason. Or, as he said, 'The script is greeeaaat! They got missiles, anti-aircraft guns, napalm, oil slicks ... it's serious stuff. Oh yes, it's right up my street.'

While the original film had been criticised for being a ser-iously bad influence on young drivers – the competing Death Racers scored points by knocking down pedestrians – this remake or sequel, made more than thirty years later, presented the central characters in a darker, more chilling setting. Roger Corman was again involved, this time as Executive Producer, but part of the great attraction for Jason was the joint British presence of film producer Jeremy Bolt and the young director Paul W. S. Anderson. Together Bolt and Anderson had worked on the incredibly successful zombie-thriller series Resident Evil, and Anderson had earlier made a name for himself with his banned and violent ram-raiding first feature Shopping. He was also married to Milla Jovovich, the Ukrainian actress and Resi-dent Evil star who had previously been wed to Jason's friend and Transporter creator, Luc Besson.

Bolt and Anderson had been absolutely determined to land Jason as the film's leading man. 'Jason is very blue-collar, which I needed for the role,' said Paul Anderson. 'And he's got a tough moral veneer to him. It's that 1970s-style vibe that I really, really liked. The young Eastwood, the young

180

'He was dead...but he got better.' Jason's Chev Chelios needs to hot wire his temporary battery-powered heart in *Crank: High Voltage*.

Jason Statham lines up with the star-studded cast of *The Expendables*.

Stallone cast Jason as Lee Christmas, a former SAS soldier, in his blockbuster *The Expendables*.

Jason arrives at the Planet Hollywood Casino Resort ready to celebrate the success of the movie.

When stunts are required, Jason steps up.

Above: Jason's beautiful girlfriend Rosie Huntington-Whiteley.

Opposite: Jason on the set of Bourne-style thriller *Safe*.

Jason with his much-deserved GQ Men of the Year Award

Bronson, the young Steve McQueen feel. And I think Jason is one of the few actors who has that in spades.'

On top of his style, another trait that attracted Anderson and Bolt to Jason was his down-to-earth, non-starry attitude – a real rarity in modern Los Angeles. As Jeremy Bolt explained, 'Jason's not *too* Hollywood. He's all the things that you want in a gritty movie and we tried to make this film gritty.'

'Not too Hollywood' extended to Jason's looks, too. The producers admired his natural athleticism and 'didn't want someone who had that kind of puffed-up LA bodybuilder look', according to Anderson: 'We wanted someone that was lean and wiry and tough. Again, getting back to what Charles Bronson looked like, what Clint Eastwood used to look like.'

It was this kind of attention to detail that made the part in *Death Race* so attractive to Jason. He was incredibly impressed with all aspects of their pre-production, and it was unlike any other film he had prepared for. 'I actually had a meeting with Paul and it was so detailed. He had pictures of the cars and completely understood the emotion of the Death Race. He knew every beat of the story and I was like, "God this man is so tuned in!"' It was critically important for Jason that both Anderson and Bolt had the track record, the right philosophy and the commitment to making the film look and feel realistic for viewers, particularly given that it was a remake.

It seems that Jason and the producers had the same aims in mind. As ever, Jason was keen to make the film seem as authentic as possible and the producers shared this desire. 'I've made lots of movies where you have tons of CG images in them,' admitted Anderson, 'but I think audiences are getting a little tired of that. When people were making movies like *Bullitt*, Walter Hill's *The Driver*, and in particular *The Road Warrior* [a.k.a. *Mad Max 2*], the car races were done for real. If you saw it onscreen it was because some stuntman had just strapped himself in a car and went and did it. There's no computer-generated imagery.'

Determined to build on the controversial reputation of the 1975 original, but intent on making a movie that was both disturbing and relevant to a 21st-century audience, Paul W. S. Anderson's *Death Race* opened with an almost-too-realistic, too-close-to-home, scary prediction of the immediate economic future: '2012. The United States' economy collapses. Unemployment hits a record high. Crime rates spiral out of control. The prison system reaches breaking point.'

Against this backdrop, Terminal Island Penitentiary was now being run for private profit and Governor Hennessey, addicted to TV ratings, was making millions by streaming cage fights between inmates over the internet and pay-per-view cable. These cage battles were fought to the death. 'They are the new Gladiators,' went the hype, 'and Terminal Island is their Coliseum.' But, as the opening scenes predicted, the audience demanded something more extreme and so 'the Death Race is born'.

Jason played the character Jensen Ames, an ex-racecar driver. The character hadn't had the easiest of upbringings, spending a lot of his life in trouble with the law, ducking in and out of prison. He had then overcome his problems and settled down with a lovely wife and baby daughter. However his domestic bliss was shattered when his wife was horrifically murdered. Jensen is framed for the crime and ended up in Terminal Island.

As Jason explained, the governor 'runs this race and all

the people within the prison make their own cars. They put in machine-guns and missiles and napalm and smoke and ejector seats. These are the most tricked-out, armour-plated *Mad Max* wreck-tech-style cars racing to the death. If you win five races, you get parole.'

The film started with the legend of the Death Race, a masked driver known as Frankenstein (voiced by David Carradine, reprising his original role) winning his fourth race but, unknown to paying viewers, dying in the process. In order to keep up the ratings of 50 million (and growing), Hennessey forced Jensen Ames (Jason) to play Frankenstein. It is later revealed that she was behind the murder of Ames' wife to ensure that he was imprisoned in Terminal Island and could drive in the Death Race.

Frankenstein, now Ames in disguise, needed only one more win and he would be freed and able to look after his child. Hennessey, of course, didn't want this to happen. She wanted to keep her star driver in Terminal Island and, as the story progressed, increased the degree of life-threatening difficulty the Death Race drivers faced. This extended to introducing the Dreadnaught, a massive beast of a truck that boasted flame-throwers, massive guns and a tank turret. Producer Jeremy Bolt compared it to a Spanish galleon, or like 'bringing on the tigers in the final Coliseum scenes of *Gladiator*'.

The cast included Joan Allen as the hard-line prison governor Hennessey, Ian McShane as Coach, and Tyrese Gibson as the fierce competitor Machine Gun Joe (Sylvester Stallone's role in the 1975 film). Joan Allen was well-known for her roles as Pam Landy in *The Bourne Ultimatum* and *The Bourne Supremacy*, while Ian McShane had made his name in award-winning TV shows such as *Lovejoy* and *Deadwood*.

Meanwhile, Jason's co-driver in *Death Race* was the husband-killer Case, played by the beautiful Latin American actress Natalie Martinez. In her first feature-film role, Martinez definitely met with Jason's approval in this ultimate movie about cars and girls. She had starred in Justin Timberlake's 'Señorita' music video, was well-known for the TV soap opera *Saints & Sinners* and had become the face of Jennifer Lopez's JLO lifestyle brand. Interviewed on set, Jason clearly felt that she was the perfect choice for *Death Race's Top Gear*-meets-lad-mag audience: 'You've got hot chicks, what more do you want?' he laughed, when asked about Martinez. 'She looks great in a crop top ... boys being boys!'

While filming *Death Race*, Jason would spend hours each day in the car with Natalie. 'What did you talk about?' asked one journalist. 'Oh, if I told you I'd have to kill you,' laughed Jason. 'No, we just talked. She is quite a funny girl. She has a lot of testosterone coursing through her veins, which just makes her quite funny. She's super-glamorous but she can mix it with the guys, have a laugh and I like girls like that. Visually stunning with a dirty mind!'

Now employed by Universal Pictures, on his first major salary in a big studio movie, Jason realised that he needed to be fighting fit to convey the physicality of Jensen Ames' role and the emotional complexities of his tragic-heroic character. In order for the film to work, *Death Race* had to be believable. The world of Terminal Island was brutally harsh, populated by the most evil and barbaric criminals American society had unfortunately created. Hardened by his wrongful conviction, and marked out as a dangerous loner amongst the fierce, territorial tribes who ran the prison, Jensen Ames needed to look as if he could survive the violence.

'It would be a sad day that a production wastes good money on CGI just to give me muscles,' Jason had said before filming, while he got into 'prison shape' fitness following a visit to California's Corcoran State Prison. After several months training with the former Navy SEAL Logan Hood, who had knocked the Spartans into shape for the 2006 battle film *300*, Jason was at the peak of his physical fitness.

Showing incredible self-discipline and commitment during this pre-production process, he compared his diet on *Death Race* with his recent experience on *The Bank Job*: 'I've just made a movie in the UK and the traditional English way of eating is something you don't want to get used to if you're going to take your shirt off in a movie.' On the *Death Race* set, while the rest of the crew ate pies and cakes, Jason would only eat cold raw vegetables, 'zero calories, zero taste'.

'He got into amazing shape for the movie, he dropped to six per cent body fat,' observed Paul Anderson. 'Jason came up to me near the end of the shoot and said "I just can't wait to drink beer and eat cake." God bless him, he didn't. During the movie he was very, very focused.' It certainly paid off on screen. As one impressed critic wrote, 'he's shredded – abs, chest and arms barbed and muscular'.

Aside from looking phenomenally fit and following a truly spartan diet, Jason was also determined to be in perfect shape to perform many of his own stunts on *Death Race*. Even though the cost of insuring him for action must have risen phenomenally in keeping with the film's big studio budget, he was determined to be actively involved.

When he had first met up with Paul W. S. Anderson ahead of filming, he had commented on the amazing designs for the various vehicles taking part in the race. The director had described the cars as harking back to the aesthetics of 1980s 'wreck-tech' film vehicles. 'The cars look bitchin',' Jason agreed. 'I wouldn't do *Death Race* to sit in my trailer while someone else drove a V8 Mustang. I went to driving school for two weeks but they still got nervous when I asked for the keys.'

In *Death Race*, Jason drove a Ford Shelby Mustang 500 complete with ejector seats, napalm and bonnet-mounted mini-guns that can fire 4,000 rounds a minute. Other custom-built, dramatically altered cars featured in the film included a Buick Riviera, Jaguar XJS and a Dodge Ram. As second unit director Spiro Razatos observed on set, 'Jason couldn't wait. He was doing the movie but he hadn't had the chance to do any action yet. After being on the stage, he just couldn't wait. He was like a tiger let out of his cage. He was doing 180-degree spins and reverse 180s, banging cars, he had a great time!'

Afterwards Jason was full of praise for the car designers and joked that some of the extra features would have been extremely useful in everyday life: 'There's times when I've actually thought "Wouldn't it be nice to have one of those mini-guns sort of sat up there on the bonnet?" You'd get yourself in all kinds of trouble if you started using those. If you saw what one of those things do ... Oh my God!'

Death Race was a visually exciting, cleverly scripted and well-executed production featuring strong performances from Jason, Ian McShane and Joan Allen. And although Jason fully realised that the bleak, gritty, over-the-top subject matter might not appeal to critics' sensitive tastes, he made his position very clear: 'This is the kind of movie I want to go and see. I mean, it's a very adult form of entertainment. It certainly plugs into what my taste is all about. This is the kind of movie that would definitely lure me into the cinema seat.' Yet again, Jason demonstrated his commitment and loyalty to his films and their producers even in the face of some negative critical reactions.

Audiences agreed with him, but only up to a point. Far from being a flop, *Death Race* returned $76million on its estimated $45million production budget. But it wasn't really helped by reviewers, who seemed to concentrate on the grim world of the story, expressing their own judgmental concerns at the way Paul W. S. Anderson's film reflected the moral decline of the cinema-going and television-watching public.

Although the *Chicago Tribune* spoke of 'our hero, a seething kettle of violence played by Jason Statham', James Berardinelli of *Reelviews* bemoaned *Death Race*'s 'attempts at satire, emphasising how bloodthirsty the human race is, paying $99 a round to watch humans getting blown up and shredded'. He suggested it was a sign of our times that this video-game-style movie was about 'mayhem on wheels, tough guys viewers can root for, and villains whose comeuppances audiences crave'.

A more accurate and representative view came in the *New York Times*, which questioned the direction Hollywood was heading generally while attempting to put *Death Race* into some kind of 21st-century screen perspective. It described the film as 'a delectable bit of B-movie savagery' and 'a supercharged junkyard apocalypse powered by an unabashed relish for brutal comeuppance and a flair for vehicular mayhem'. More importantly, for Jason's career, it concluded that 'anchored by the ever-dependable Mr Statham and his gruff buff stoicism, the movie is legitimately greasy, authentically nasty, with a good old-fashioned sense of laying waste to everything in sight – including the shallow philosophising and computer-generated fakery that has over-run the summer blockbuster'.

It wasn't surprising to hear Jason referred to as 'ever-dependable' around the time of *Death Race*'s release in September 2008. Even though it was exactly ten years since the launch of Guy Ritchie's *Lock Stock & Two Smoking Barrels*, he had become a permanent fixture in Hollywood and was rightly now being billed as 'the biggest action star in Tinseltown'. But while he had clearly enjoyed the *Death Race* experience and working with Paul W. S. Anderson and Jeremy Bolt, when Universal Pictures demanded a follow-up, Jason felt in-demand enough and sufficiently empowered to turn down the lucrative project. *Death Race 2010* would instead go into production with Sean Bean and Luke Goss (of Bros) in the driving seats.

Throughout this experience as the leading man in his first big Hollywood studio production, Jason had developed greater confidence in his own abilities and, importantly, in his own judgement when it came to deciding which film projects to get involved with. 'I feel like I know what I'm doing now,' he said, 'and what it takes to make a good movie. So I feel more educated. I have a lot more knowledge on the whole process of how a movie gets made and the process of that.'

There was nothing arrogant about this new-found sense of certainty. He was the first to admit that 'I'm not Tom Cruise or Brad Pitt!' and in interviews he self-deprecatingly seemed to accept the criticism that he had got lucky in some respects, but he also argued that – in an incredibly short space of time – he had also worked extremely hard and made the very best of his diverse talents. He had always been honest about his good fortune and the opportunities he had been given, particularly through close associates such as Jet Li, Corey Yuen, manager Steve Chasman, and his writer/ director friends Guy Ritchie and Luc Besson. *The Transporter*, in particular, had acted as the perfect showreel and shop window for his martial arts, stunt-driving and potential action-hero strengths.

Yet again, Jason attributed his success to authenticity, commitment and hands-on experience. 'If you've got a good imagination, a lot of confidence and you kind of know what you are saying, then you might be able to do it,' he told one interviewer. 'I know a lot of colourful characters at home that would make great actors. I'm slowly learning and getting my experience first-hand, if you like, without any training or whatever, and the more you do, the more you learn.'

The more you learn and, particularly in Jason's case, the more you *earn*. He had reportedly received salaries of $450,000 in 2003 for his supporting role as Handsome Rob in *The Italian Job* and $750,000 for starring in the first of the *Transporter* films back in 2002. It had sounded like big money at the time, but by 2008 these fees would be the equivalent of small change.

Although he would understandably keep his financial affairs private from the mid-2000s onwards, it is rumoured that he earned in the region of $5million for *Death Race* alone. By the end of the decade it was predicted that Jason would soon become the first $20million-a-film British action star. Not bad for a bloke who, twenty years earlier, had struggled to fund an amateur diving career by selling fake jewellery and perfume on street corners.

Already, by 2008, his standard of living had exceeded all

his wildest dreams. In addition to his home in London, since 2005 he had owned a 2,281-square-foot house in LA's Hollywood Hills, which he apparently bought for $2.4million (£1.6million), and from September 2008 he would also own a two-bedroom apartment in the Broadway building in the heart of Hollywood. He put this up for sale in September 2009, however, when paying $11million (£7.3million) to purchase a 3,355-square-foot ocean-front house in the exclusive Malibu colony of California. According to the estate agent's description, 'The main house features three bedrooms, an ocean-front sitting area, a gourmet kitchen and a guest apartment with another two bedrooms.'

Jay Leno, the US chat-show host, asked him if it was the legendary Johnny Carson's old home, but Jason denied this: 'It's not actually Johnny Carson's house. That's bad information. But it's down there on the beach.'

In fact, Jason bought the luxury beach home from the movie producer Matt Palmieri, and found that his new neighbours included Tom Hanks, Jim Carrey, Sting, Pamela Anderson and the billionaire socialite and philanthropist Wallis Annenberg. 'Will you be going round asking for biscuits or a cup of sugar?' asked Jay Leno. 'I ain't borrowing bones for gravy,' laughed Jason.

But Jason was not one to boast about his luxury life, let alone flaunt his wealth in photo-shoots for celebrity magazines such as *OK* or *Hello*. In interviews, he made his everyday life away from movie shoots sound almost mundane, explaining how he rarely socialised unless he was either back in London, or spending time with family or trusted friends.

When he was in LA, however, he sometimes found himself rubbing shoulders with expat Brits in Hollywood. For example, one day at the Chateau Marmont – the famous West Hollywood hotel off Sunset Boulevard, once frequented by legends such as Judy Garland, Elizabeth Taylor, Greta Garbo, Jim Morrison and John Belushi (who died there in 1982) – Jason bumped into Paul McKenna, the hypnotist. McKenna told Jason, '"I live on your street, come to my barbecue." So I went there', recalled Jason, 'and there were all these Brits there like Jonny Lee Miller and Cat Deeley.'

In fact, he would not spend many weekends in Los Angeles hanging out with Hollywood's new British recruits. Jason admitted that the barbeque at Paul McKenna's was 'the first time in five years I have spent an afternoon mixing with a group of British people', stating that 'Usually I just kick around with Vinnie Jones and Guy Ritchie. They keep my feet on the ground.'

In American interviews he has often sounded nostalgic for the real or imagined Britain he left behind, perhaps fearing that the exclusive LA air he was now breathing might be affecting him as a person. 'LA's great but London's my real home,' he'd tell Jay Leno. 'I'm always looking forward to going back and seeing my friends and family. They'd be the first people to tell if I'd changed and gone *too Hollywood.*'

Whether he was longing for the simpler, less complicated life he had experienced in London in the 1990s – perhaps the blissful early years of his relationship with Kelly Brook – we will most likely never know. At one point, amusingly, in an American bar he had even seemed to regret the lack of an old-style British boozer brawl. 'They run out to the car and get their pistol from the glove compartment,' he complained. 'There's no such thing as a proper pub fight here.'

Even though, professionally, Jason was now approaching

the action-adventure-hero popularity and status of 1980s big guns such as Harrison Ford, Mel Gibson, Arnold Schwarzenegger, Sylvester Stallone and Bruce Willis, in personal terms he still seemed to be struggling to fill the chasm that Kelly Brook had left in his life. His intense commitment to work – his desire to develop as an all-round actor and his focused determination to grow as a film star – had clearly made it difficult for him to settle down again. Juggling life between different homes and different continents can't have helped the situation either.

'I do like California,' he explained. 'It's a great place, but I'm never in one place long enough to say this is where I want to make my home. When I get sick of one I go to the other. Hollywood's a desperate town; people are obsessed with the industry, and there's all the horrible bullshit that goes with that, so it's hard to find a nice girl. But Brits walk around hanging their heads and moaning all day. So you just can't win.'

Since the high level of media intrusion that had marked the end of his seven-year relationship with Kelly Brook in September 2004, Jason had avoided being photographed in public with prospective new partners. There had been points in his film career when – free and single, living the bachelor life – he was clearly enjoying himself again. For example, while on location in Vancouver he told the Canadian press, 'I love it. It's a great part of the world. So many beautiful ladies. You grow them well up here.'

It seemed ironic that, when he had first found success in films, he was in a settled relationship and leading a relatively domestic life with Kelly. Now, an incredibly wealthy movie-star pin-up, in the prime of his life and with all the trappings of fame, he struggled to find the right woman to share the experience. Clearly he would have plenty of fun searching.

While filming the art-house feature film *London* in 2005, Jason had a relationship with the blonde actress and singer Sophie Monk. Born in England but brought up in Australia, Sophie had found fame as a member of Bardot, a band created on the *Popstars* TV series in 1999. She had been a Marilyn Monroe impersonator in a TV film called *The Mystery of Natalie Wood* and would later appear in *Date Movie* and *Click* with Adam Sandler. Jason and Sophie were together for several months after filming *London*, during which time they hung out with co-stars Chris Evans and his then partner Jessica Biel (who had also both been in *Cellular* with Jason).

A British tabloid reported an unnamed source telling them, on 3 October 2005, 'Jason was shocked when Kelly walked out and didn't have the decency to tell him. But he's not so sore now the offers are rolling in and he's seeing Sophie. They get on really well and, although it's early days, everyone has noticed how happy he is.'

After splitting with Sophie, Jason's girlfriend for almost two years until spring 2010 was the LA socialite Alex Zosman. However, because of Jason's pressing work commitments and his international filming schedule during this period – seven leading roles in major movies including *The Bank Job*, *Death Race*, *Transporter 3*, and *Crank 2: High Voltage* – the relationship never seemed to be permanent. They were often photographed on holiday together but, perhaps tellingly, he never talked openly about their affair in interviews. All he would tell the Australian press, in July 2008, was that 'I've got a girl I'm knocking around with, but I'm not going to talk about my private life.'

He was determined to keep the press at arm's distance and protect his privacy. Few photographers risked the fearsome wrath of 'The Stath', as he was now becoming respectfully known. He was certainly not the type of celebrity to be seen living it large in the magnesium flashlights of the paparazzi. In fact, he had even allegedly shunned an opportunity to be photographed with some of the most beautiful girls in Los Angeles.

Without much supporting evidence, Jason would – at various points – be linked with a variety of beautiful and famous women, including Denise van Outen and Pamela Anderson. He had only been spotted having a curry in London with Van Outen, Kelly Brook's predecessor on the *Big Breakfast*, and he denied even knowing Anderson. 'I've never even said hello to Pam,' he responded to claims that they were romantically involved. 'The closest I've got to her was being in the same room at a *Vanity Fair* party.' He would also deny dating the Playboy model Holly Madison and George Clooney's ex-girlfriend Sarah Lawson after they were pictured together in Las Vegas. 'I have met her,' Jason said in July 2008. 'I was in Vegas with my friend and manager Steve Chasman last week and we were all at a big table. Next thing you know I'm supposed to be jumping in and out of bed with her.'

However, one actress whose company he clearly enjoyed was the star of US reality TV show *The Hills*, Kristin Cavallari. Sometimes billed as a 'controversy magnet', the blonde actress had appeared in *Cheerleader Camp*, *Wild Cherry* and also *Laguna Beach: The Real Orange County*. Although according to *US Weekly* their relationship was 'not serious ... it's a hook-up situation', Jason and Kristin had been spotted out several times in Hollywood and would share an interesting ride in Indio, California after the Coachella music festival. Jason and Kristin had been partying hard when, in the early hours of the morning, the Palm Springs Police allegedly stopped them driving along the main road in a stolen golf cart. They were quietly reprimanded, told to return the buggy and go back to their hotel.

Despite the rumoured relationships and his many platonic friendships with a variety of beautiful women, Jason was still with Alex Zosman in January 2010 on a New Year Caribbean holiday, having just completed *Transporter 3* and *Crank 2*. Spotted in St. Barts, they were spending time on Harvey Weinstein's multi-million-pound yacht with friends Orlando Bloom and Miranda Kerr.

The company Jason was now keeping proved how successful he had become. The incredibly wealthy and powerful Weinstein had founded the film company Miramax, had won a producer Oscar for the *Lord of the Rings* trilogy and had also been behind many major films including Quentin Tarantino's *Pulp Fiction* and *Inglourious Basterds*. Weinstein had also worked with Sylvester Stallone on *Rambo* and clearly admired Jason's work in the action-adventure genre.

As if to further impress Weinstein, and to prove in real life that he really could do the on-screen stunts he had now become internationally famous for, Jason executed a perfect dive from the top deck of Harvey's yacht, arrowing down into the Caribbean sea 25 feet below. A celebrity photographer just happened to be there to capture the moment.

If, by 2009, Kelly Brook had been the only major love of Jason's adult life, then things began to change for the actor in March 2010, when he was spotted together with a new partner, first at South Kensington's Brompton Club in London and secondly at the Coachella Festival in California in April. Naturally, the tabloid press went into overdrive to secure pictures of his latest flame – the model Rosie Huntington-Whiteley.

At twenty-three years of age – fifteen years Jason's junior – Rosie's beauty had been celebrated by the famous photographer Rankin, who had declared 'she's already the next supermodel'. Huntington-Whiteley, who had modelled for Burberry, Pirelli and Victoria's Secret, later turned her hand to acting, with a lead role in *Transformers 3*, following in the footsteps of Megan Fox. The *Sunday Times* created an appetising verbal portrait of her: 'Those unmistakable lips, like two freshly plumped hotel pillows. The slanted blue eyes that verge on feline. The long, blonde glamour-puss hair. And that body: the long limbs, the washboard stomach, the pert breasts we've come to see a lot of in recent years. The whole package has helped Rosie Huntington-Whiteley embody our most coveted ideal of beauty – a quietly flushed perfection that hints at still waters running deep.'

Having previously dated Tyrone Wood (son of Rolling Stones and Faces guitarist Ronnie) and Kylie Minogue's ex-boyfriend Olivier Martinez, Rosie told the *Sunday Times* that – without mentioning Jason by name – she was now 'so in love, I'm very happy'. The romance had developed quickly. On 21 April 2010, the *Daily Mail* reported that 'Jason Statham looked like the cat who's got the cream as he stepped out in Los Angeles with Rosie Huntington-Whiteley yesterday.' The paper went on to claim that Jason 'took his new love to Cartier during their shopping spree', but added that there was still no engagement ring in sight.

Later newspaper reports, in the summer of 2010, suggested that Rosie would move in with Jason and that, despite his ongoing occasional social contact with old girlfriend Kelly Brook, this would be the major new relationship in Jason's life. In October, the *Daily Mail* reported that while Jason was filming *Safe* in New York, he and Rosie were considering buying an apartment in the exclusive Richard Meier buildings in Greenwich Village, home to Jim Carrey and Hugh Jackman.

With the multi-million-dollar film career, the fantastic homes in the USA and UK, the loyal support of family and friends, and the 'coveted ideal of beauty' that is Rosie Huntington-Whiteley, it is hard to imagine how reality could get much better for Jason Statham. Set up for life but with the most rewarding years of movie stardom perhaps still ahead of him, he was ready to indulge in his passion for classic cars.

Cars have played an important part in most of his action movies, from *The Transporter* through to *Death Race*, and earlier in his career he had often spoken about his love of vehicles and his ambition to buy a big house with a large garage so that he could start collecting. 'I've always had a fascination with cars and racing,' he'd told *Auto Trader* magazine. 'I think most men are interested in speed ... more so than flower-arranging.'

So what is Jason's car of choice? The *Independent* had once reported that 'Statham loves Audis. He owns two of them. Drives them in the *Transporter* films. Starred in a Superbowl ad for them. Even narrated a documentary about them.' Indeed, the first fast car he bought was an Audi RS6 – a four-door family car with twin turbo V8 engine and 450hp – followed by an Audi S8 450hp sedan. 'I'm into all things

German,' he once told the *Female First* website. 'Everything I own is German. As far as cars go, anyway. I drive an Audi, an S8.'

Before *The Italian Job*, Jason had listed some of his favourite vehicles – the old Aston Martins, the BB5s, early Jags such as the XK120 and E-Types – and said that if or when he had the money, 'I'd probably buy the Aston Martin, or a luxury car like the Bentley would be cool. I do like the sports cars.' And Jason wasn't beyond admiring other people's cars: 'One of the members of Jamiroquai has just bought a new Ferrari called, I think, the Enzo. Have you seen it? It's, like, unbelievable. It looks like a rocket!'

Although he hadn't done much driving on location in *War* with Jet Li in 2007, he had joked that all the fancy cars were being used by villains such as Shiro (played by Ryo Ishibashi), and complained, 'You'll see Jet scooting about in a very nice one, but I've got an old muscle car, a Chevelle.' By 2008 he was driving a GT2 Porsche or Porsche 911; at the time, one of the fastest cars ever built. While the high quality of his stunt driving remained one of his great professional assets, he also found competitive racing strangely relaxing.

'I go to a track called Willow Springs where you can hammer it,' Jason said. 'I've been up there with Lamborghinis and Ferraris and for me it is the best track in the world. You get a street-car with plenty of juice and go and hammer it around a track for an afternoon; it's a lot of fun. There is always a corner coming up on that track, though, so you're never too much above 140–145 mph.'

But it wasn't a solo social pleasure. There needed to be a competitive element to his sport: 'I love to get behind the wheel and get competitive. I've always had that competitive nature, whether racing around the track in Mini Coopers or diving off a platform or doing a bit of grappling. Whatever it is, I've got that competitive edge.'

Another of his action hero skills, his stuntman disciplines, had also become a professional and personal passion. On-screen, in the mould of Clint Eastwood and Sylvester Stallone, Jason looked as if he'd been born with a gun in his hand. Whether as a cop in *Chaos* or an FBI agent in *War*, he seemed believably comfortable in possession of firearms. Perhaps this was because he often got together in Los Angeles to shoot with industry friends such as Brad Pitt, Guy Ritchie and Vinnie Jones, or with *Crank* film-makers Brian Taylor and Mark Neveldine. In one interview, while firing a .50-calibre Smith & Wesson, he had put on a comedy voice and snarled, 'This nasty gun will knock the frost off an old granny.'

Jason particularly enjoyed the training for these scenes and revealed, 'We all go to a range downtown, pin up the target, get the old .44 Magnum out and bang, bang, bang *Dirty Harry*-style. Then you get the little SIG-Sauer, the Glock, the AK47, the Desert Eagle ... You just blast away on any gun you want. It's great fun and I can't get injured.'

Despite this fascination with guns, however, Jason stood firmly against the American way of life concerning the widespread use of firearms, and had no problem separating the real world from the unreal existence of his film characters. Defending Britain, the land of his birth, he told the *New York Times* in 2010, 'I'm happy to live in a country where you're not allowed to keep a gun under your mattress.'

In 2009, Jason's interest in guns may have been one of the reasons he had decided to appear as a bowler-hatted gambler in Géla Babluani's film *13*. Strangely, the acclaimed young Georgian director now found himself in Hollywood making an American version of his own deeply dark and shocking thriller *13 Tzameti*, which had won a 'Special Jury Prize' at the Sundance Film Festival in 2007 and had also picked up a 'Best First Film' award at the Venice Film Festival. Starring the director's younger brother George Babluani as an impoverished Georgian immigrant living in France, *13 Tzameti* looked at the lives of desperate men who agreed to take part in loaded-gun games of Russian roulette for the sick amusement and excitement of wealthy gamblers. It was a bit like *Death Race* but with pistols.

One of Géla Babluani's many admirers, David Kohl of Palm Pictures, had hailed *13 Tzameti* as 'a true discovery. It's a mix of *Rifiki*, *Man Bites Dog* and *Fight Club*. The cinematography is powerful and the images stay with you for a long time.' Shot in grainy, high-contrast black and white, Babluani's original presented a bleak and depressing portrait of humanity in which the rich made or lost money betting on the miserably cheap lives of thirteen competitors, who all stood in a circle holding a gun – each with one live bullet in a barrel of six – to the head of the man alongside him.

Having made his original film for only $10,000, Géla Babluani had managed to generate over $120,000 in income on the international film circuit. But, as the remake *13* proved, a Hollywood budget and an all-star cast including Jason, Mickey Rourke, Ray Winstone, Ben Gazzara, Curtis Jackson (a.k.a. 50 Cent) and Sam Riley (from Anton Corbijn's *Control*) would not necessarily guarantee a great picture. Shot in colour, many would be disappointed that *13* lacked the high tension and mentally disturbing commercial and critical impact of the original. Somehow, it failed to reproduce the chilling, hard-to-watch-but-fascinating quality of the earlier version.

Although too brief, the cameos from Jason Statham and Mickey Rourke were among the strengths of the film. But given the darkness of the subject matter, it was funny to hear Mickey Rourke's tales of the off-screen relationship between Jason and veteran actor Ben Gazzara. 'So we're on set,' laughed Mickey, 'and we hear "JASON!", and it's Ben four trailers away. And Jason, like *The Transporter*, runs over there. And Ben says, "I want an egg sandwich with mayo and bacon, and milk!"' Mickey Rourke admitted that he had admired Ben Gazzara's gumption but didn't confirm whether or not Jason actually transported the sandwich order. However, Rourke did say of Gazzara, 'He comes to life on camera. When they say "Action", he's right there. The rest of the time, he's somewhere else.'

Jason's involvement in *13* had only been a minor detour on his continued climb to the top of the Hollywood ladder. He had been dramatically impressive in *The Bank Job* and physically awesome in *Death Race*, and with *Transporter 3* and *Crank 2* building on his cult following in cinemas and on DVD, all of the major LA studios now wanted a piece of this action man. Coincidentally, it would be a surprise telephone call from one of the stars of the original *Death Race 2000* which would trigger the next stage of Jason's explosive acting career.

CHAPTER TEN:

HOLLYWOOD HERO

In 2008, Sheila Roberts of *Movies Online* had told Jason Statham that one of his heroes, Sylvester Stallone, predicted Jason would be his natural successor in action-adventure films. However, at the same time, Stallone had also claimed that Rambo could take the Transporter any day. The latter comment was clearly in response to a misreported quote from Jason saying he thought ageing action stars such as Sylvester Stallone should retire.

'I never said that,' replied Jason. 'I think he's great. He's one of my bloody heroes! I love all his stuff and the fact that he can still do it in his sixties is amazing. I've always liked Sly's sense of humour, but you know, the fact that he's even talking about me makes me very happy. I mean, I've watched his movies for years, and to think that he would even know who I was would be very cool.'

Roberts then suggested that maybe Jason should fight

Rocky in film seven or eight of the franchise. 'Me and Rocky, huh?' Jason laughed. 'I'm not bad. I'm better without the gloves, though. One glove on and one glove off to make us both happy.'

Being talked about in the same breath as Sly Stallone must have convinced Jason he had finally made the A-list. Even if that had been the final summit of his film career, the peak of his star status, it would still have been an extraordinary achievement given his lack of dramatic training and the journey he had made in such a short period of time. He was now one of the biggest action-adventure stars on the planet. If he needed further affirmation or confirmation, it came when the telephone rang one morning.

'I got a call and was asked if I'd have something to eat with Sylvester Stallone because he wanted to talk to me about a film,' Jason recalled, almost in a state of disbelief. Talking of his hero, Jason said, 'He is like cinema god! I grew up watching films like *Rambo* and *Rocky*. I think Sly is as big as they come. He is the most recognised film star in the world. That's why I got so excited about doing this film.' As Jason later said to chat-show host Jay Leno, 'If Sly had asked me to cut his grass, I'd have done that.'

The film, which would be called *The Expendables*, was being produced by Planet Hollywood chairman Robert Earl and would be distributed by Jason's 'home' company, Lionsgate. Impressively, Jason and his old pal Jet Li were the first actors that Sylvester Stallone approached to join the ensemble cast. 'At first it was just myself, Jason and Jet Li and it began to build from that,' Stallone said. 'As I started getting other characters at one time I thought about Ben Kingsley as the bad guy and Forest Whitaker, but I didn't think it would fly.'

At that point, Sly thought about recruiting other action movie legends, including Dolph Lundgren, his old adversary from the *Rocky* films: 'I thought about going really old-school and so I called up Dolph and he accepted immediately. But then I said, "You know there aren't a lot of bad asses out there today." ... So that's why I went to MMA [Mixed Martial Arts] and got a five-time world champion, who was really ferocious, and Steve Austin is an incredibly powerful human being – big, 250 pounds of solid muscle.'

At the age of sixty-four, Sylvester Stallone had no idea if he would be able to attract a strong enough cast of action heroes past and present. The lack of 21st-century 'bad asses', apart from Jason, naturally led to an over-dependence on old-school action heroes. Nevertheless, Stallone and Statham were both thrilled that so many action film legends agreed to be involved.

'The thing was to find certain personalities and put them all together like a dream team,' said Stallone, 'I wanted to do a film a bit like *The Magnificent Seven* or *The Dirty Dozen*. One of those that only comes along once in a while.'

The idea of creating a dream-team action movie had clearly been inspired by the great male ensemble films of Sylvester Stallone's youth. Born in 1946, the 'Italian Stallion' would have been fourteen years old when John Sturges' great Western *The Magnificent Seven* rode into the picture houses of his home city, New York. Featuring an all-star Hollywood cast of strong men including Yul Brynner, Eli Wallach, James Coburn, Robert Vaughn, Charles Bronson and Steve McQueen, *The Magnificent Seven* would act as something of a template for *The Expendables*.

But there were plenty of other movies in the 1960s and

1970s that would also inspire Stallone to gather together an attractive cast of 'bad ass' personalities. Robert Aldrich's *The Dirty Dozen* (1967) and Sam Peckinpah's *The Wild Bunch* (1969) were both films in the mould of *The Magnificent Seven*. Aldrich's Oscar-winning cast of World War II mavericks included Lee Marvin, Charles Bronson, Ernest Borgnine, Robert Ryan, Telly Savalas and Donald Sutherland. Sam Peckinpah's unromantic, gritty Western also featured Borgnine and Ryan, acting with William Holden and Warren Oates.

In the same vein, more stars gathered in 1970 for Brian G. Hutton's Hollywood war comedy *Kelly's Heroes*, in which Donald Sutherland and Telly Savalas battled alongside Clint Eastwood. And there was also a very British equivalent, in 1978, when Richard Burton, Roger Moore and Richard Harris joined forces for *The Wild Geese*, an *Expendables*-style film detailing a mercenary plot to overthrow an African dictator.

Stallone's 'dream team' idea clearly appealed to Jason, too. 'I really liked the concept,' he said, 'all these regular guys with insecurities and problems of their own. At the same time, when they're put in a situation where they need to focus and kick butt, they can all do that. It's a testosterone-fuelled line-up, as you'll realise when you see the motley crew that Sly's assembled.'

Regardless of age and experience, the diversely talented ensemble cast of *The Expendables* was impressive. Sylvester Stallone cast himself as Barney Ross, the leader of this mercenary, 'if-the-money's-right' gang, while Jason played his younger apprentice, the knife-wielding Lee Christmas. Jet Li was the martial artist Yin Yang, UFC fighter Randy Couture signed up for the role of Toll Road, the Demolition Man, while Mickey Rourke gladly parodied himself as a gone-to-seed tattoo artist called Tool. Alongside them, there was Dolph Lundgren's mad, dangerous Gunner Jensen – echoing his unhinged role as Rocky's arch-enemy Ivan Drago – top real-life wrestler 'Stone Cold' Steve Austin, plus Terry Crews as the comedic Hale Caesar, a weapons expert. It was no wonder that one newspaper branded them as 'a veritable who's who of Hollywood bad boys and muscle-men'.

As if this impressive assemblage of ancient action heroes (plus a few fresh fighters) wasn't enough to lure a wider audience into cinemas, Stallone then called in cameo favours from two of his old great 1980s screen rivals and Planet Hollywood partners: Bruce Willis as Mr Church and California Governor Arnold Schwarzenegger as Mr Tench. There would be an affectionate and amusing scene early on in which Willis' shady Mr Church had to decide whether to give the lucrative mercenary contract to either Ross (Stallone) or to Tench (Schwarzenegger). 'Give it to my friend,' said Arnie, referring to old Rambo, 'he loves playing in the jungle.'

Aside from representatives of the next generation of action stars – such as Jason's contemporaries Vin Diesel, Dwayne Johnson and Wesley Snipes – *The Expendables'* cast list only lacked the presence of Steven Seagal and Jean-Claude Van Damme.

Van Damme later explained to *Total Film* magazine why he had refused a role that could have potentially put him back on the action-adventure map: 'Stallone gave me a part in his next movie. But I ask him about the subject, about the story. He said, "You're gonna make lots of money." I don't want to hear that, I want to hear about my character. He was unable to tell me so I didn't do the movie.'*

When the cast was announced, the question on everyone's lips was how the hell had Stallone afforded to pay them? In order to pay the huge sums involved, he had relied on favours and the years of goodwill he had built up. 'A lot of it was calling in,' Sly laughed. 'I could never afford Bruce Willis and Arnold Schwarzenegger in the same movie. That would have been the whole budget. Jason's a lot of money ... but well worth a £100 a week. Seriously! Whereas some people might have been getting $10million a few years ago, now they're down to about $2million and they're going, "Thank you!" But this was all done on favours, on a really low budget.'

At an estimated $80million the budget wasn't that low but, as Stallone revealed, the workings of the major studios had changed dramatically since he, Willis, Schwarzenegger, Rourke and Lundgren had first stepped out as Statham-like young action heroes. Recalling that Hollywood studios had once produced about 400 films a year, he now revealed that the credit-crunch output was down to around 150. This increased the pressure on each film to perform, and raised expectations at the box office. 'The stakes are really high and it's become a science on what the studios make. Every actor is weighed up against what he's going to bring in from the territories. It's like a maths project, it really is.'

Working on this maths-project theory, it wasn't hard to

* Stallone had also tried to enlist his old *Tango & Cash* sidekick Kurt Russell but, disappointingly, had failed to get past Russell's agent who told him that Kurt wasn't interested in 'ensemble acting'.

see why Jason Statham had received the first call from Sly and would get second billing below Stallone on the film posters. Of the Magnificent Nine central characters – Steve Austin, Randy Couture, Dolph Lundgren, Jet Li, Sylvester Stallone, Terry Crews, Mickey Rourke, Bruce Willis and Jason Statham – only Jason and Jet Li could be counted on to bring in younger, diverse audiences from different territories. The rest of the cast, branded the 'fossils with muscles', all looked like they'd been through the Hollywood mincer several times.

Stallone – as wise as his years and as shrewd as a still-working sexagenarian Hollywood action hero writer-director needed to be – was the first to recognise what Jason offered *The Expendables*: 'I didn't identify with John Wayne growing up, I identified with James Dean. You have to find your own heroes and this generation has defined superheroes as their heroes, so that's why we're kind of like a novelty. That's the way it is, film changes. Look at music, it's unrecognisable from twenty years ago. But maybe they'll go retro. Jason is current so that's kind of lucky for us.'

As he had done in the final *Rocky* and *Rambo* films, like a sorcerer handing over to his apprentice, Stallone presented himself as a father figure to Jason's character in *The Expendables*. 'It's very intentional,' Sly replied, when questioned on this. 'You have to be age-appropriate and Jason would be the protégé. So I tease him a bit, especially about his love life and taking himself too seriously ... the type of stuff a father and son might do.' But it wasn't just a one-sided paternal relationship. It was clear that Jason really looked up to his action-hero mentor. As he said of Stallone, 'A lot of people you put on a pedestal, those big celebrities, they're not everything you expect. But he's everything you hoped him to be. He's twice the man, he's so funny, and it's a privilege to meet somebody like that. He's the best man to take to the boozer.'

On and off screen, it was a fascinating relationship, between the old champion – still hanging on like a punch-drunk contender – and the young pretender. But Stallone also had the additional challenge of directing his *Expendables* co-stars. It would be an understatement to say that it wasn't easy. As Sly confessed, 'You get these strong men who have a certain way of doing things on a film, and you have to get them to give that up. You could feel the wattage; there is a definite heat that comes off special people. Like Jason in this film is totally different than in anything he's ever done. Dolph Lundgren is totally different.'

Jason himself later gave an insight into the competitive heat and wattage on the set of *The Expendables*. 'You can't compete with those guys,' he told Jay Leno. 'If I was in the gym doing my heaviest weights they'd come in, lift it with one hand and start warming up with it!'

Directing a group of such physically powerful, and com-petitive, men cannot have been a simple matter, and only someone with Stallone's charisma and experience could have managed the situation so well. As Sly noted, 'Guys are very aggressive. Let's say Jason does an action beat and he's very physical. You'll see it on the documentary that his hands are on ice and then he's leaping onto baked ground over and over again. He keeps wanting to do it, and I have to say "Stop!" But then the next person to do the stunt says, "Jason was rather good, I'm going to kill this guy!" So it keeps building competitiveness, which is why it feels like such a testosterone-driven movie. Men are just naturally competitive and they want to keep upping the ante. You had to be tough to be on this show.'

Speaking on the USA's *Lopez Tonight* chat-show, Jason admitted that being one part of such a strong line-up was intimidating. He admits, 'It's the first movie I've been in that I've felt like a pussy. They're like the meatheads. It's good to make a lot of friends on that kind of film set. I was on my best behaviour . . . I get to work with a lot of good people and this is probably the biggest and best one I've done in a long time.'

The film's old-fashioned, corny shock-jock-voiced trailer set the tone perfectly: 'They are the world's greatest mercenaries . . . the only life they've ever known . . . is war . . . the only loyalty they've ever had . . . is to each other.'

The plot of *The Expendables*, which earned closer comparisons with *The Wild Geese* rather than *The Wild Bunch*, wasn't simple in a 1980s way. The gang of old mercenaries Barney Ross reassembled all seemed to have developed flaws with age, or personal problems had eaten away at their respective talents. Initially, they defeated Somalian pirates intent on executing hostages, but soon found themselves in the more traditional terrain of action heroes and covert US foreign policy territory; invading the island of Vilena and attempting to depose a ruthless Caribbean dictator General Garza (played by David Zayas), who was backed by a rogue CIA agent James Munroe (Eric Roberts).

The moral and romantic dilemma, at least for Stallone's character Barney, was whether or not he should lead his unruly mercenaries on a suicide mission to save the life of Garza's idealistic and attractive daughter Sandra (Giselle Itié). Whenever the Expendables entered the fray, whipping up blizzards of violence, surviving intense shoot-outs, bloodily defeating the combined forces of evil, the film echoed with elements of Stallone's *Rambo* heroics, humorously paid homage to classic pictures from *The Magnificent Seven* through to the *Last Action Hero*, but still allowed Jason to star in several amazing stunts including a memorable attack on an enemy port in an old war plane.

The war plane stunt was an illustration of Stallone's confidence in Jason, and perhaps also proved that Sly, the old warrior, wasn't personally prepared to take too many risks any more. As Jason told Jay Leno on the *Tonight Show*, 'That was supposed to be Sly in the nose of the plane and he changed the stunt. I was supposed to be doing another one and he changed it on the day of the stunt.' Doing a perfect gruff impression of Stallone, Jason continued, 'He went "Jay Jay Jay … I gotta new idea, it's gonna be better for your character, I want you to do the plane thing, it's all gonna be great." So I'm like, "Whatever you want Sly … no problem". Anyway, we do the stunt. We come down at the end of the day and I say to the pilot, "Was that OK?" And the pilot said, "Yeah we was having a lot of problems with the plane. You're lucky we stayed up in the air. We've had engine trouble and there was oil leaking out of it."'

'So Stallone knew this and he put *you* in the plane?' laughed Jay Leno.

'Yep, he put the new guy in the plane,' replied Jason. 'The plane was sixty years old, barely airworthy! It hadn't been serviced for about thirty years. Sly wanted to bring it in for the premiere but we found out it had been crushed into a cube.'

As Lee Christmas, the former SAS soldier who specialised

in close-quarter combat with knives, Jason dominated proceedings with Stallone and, charismatically, seemed to have most of the screen time. Arguably, the only believable male/female on-film chemistry in *The Expendables* was between Christmas and his ex-girlfriend Lacey. Certainly, the most trailed scene featured Jason single-handedly outfighting Lacey's thuggish boyfriend and his ugly gang on a basketball court. At the end of the fight, with the bad guys strewn on the ground, Christmas takes his knife and bursts the basketball on the boyfriend's chest, growling 'Next time I'll deflate all your balls.'

Charisma Carpenter – who played Lacey and who had previously starred in the cult TV series *Buffy the Vampire Slayer* and *Angel* – spoke enthusiastically about her romantic moment with Jason. Talking of their on-screen kiss, she recalled 'Yes, it's him kissing me ... I can't get hold of him and he shows up unexpectedly and it's not a good time and we end up having a little bit of a fight.' Did she get to slap him, one journalist asked: 'No, I didn't even get to slap him, he nearly ran me over with his motorcycle though!'

For all the criticisms that would be made of *The Expendables* – mainly by reviewers who seemed to dislike the adventure genre in the first place, or felt that the whole idea was too much of a throwback to the 1980s – few could fault the dramatic direction of the action sequences. Jason, in particular, was impressed with Stallone's shooting style. 'The good thing about the way the movies get made when Sly's doing it is that he shoots a lot of the stunts in the camera. A lot of the action directors of today tend to rely on the movie as a visual. So it becomes very boring because there's a lot of CG and you don't really care too much about it. So when you're doing an action movie that requires real men doing real action, it's an opportunity to do that. And that's what we're looking for. We can't wait to get stuck in and do that stuff.'

It spoke volumes for Jason's personality and his ego that, despite his star billing in publicity for *The Expendables*, he talked in an extremely humble and affectionate manner about his co-stars. He fully realised that he had found himself in action hero dreamland, working with the major figures of the genre.

How did he find working with Stallone as both the star and the director? 'Well Sly's a bit of a bully, actually ... he carries a big stick around and starts ordering tea and coffee,' laughed Jason, but it was clearly a positive experience and the pair struck up quite a friendship. Jason added 'It's a situation that you get to know the real man behind the camera. It's not the film actor anymore, it's a regular guy, and to me that was the best part about getting to work with Sly. It was getting to know him as a person. There's no substitute for that. That's the great thing about having a guy who is a writer, a director and the star of the movie as well because you have full liberty to change and improvise ... you don't normally get that. You usually get restrictions where some guy wrote the script and he doesn't want anyone to mess with that, and the director isn't allowed to. So it's the best situation you can get. And the humour arises from that.'

With such a top-quality action-adventure cast, and a workable if old-fashioned dictator-toppling plot, the only great pressure on Stallone and his 'mercenary' cast would be to recoup and return on the $80million budget. 'It's a lot of pressure,' admitted Stallone. 'Sometimes you come up with a film, and you know you've got a turkey and it's not even Thanksgiving. It's bad. But this time, this is the other end of it where there's a great expectancy and you say to yourself, "Jeez, I didn't really expect this when we started making it. Is this going to live up to people's idea of it?" So it's kind of complex. You're damned if you do, you're damned if you don't.'

'Well, it's all on Sly I'm afraid,' laughed Jason when asked the same question about pressure. While, ultimately, the buck would stop with Stallone, Jason was the first to express his complete confidence in his writer, director, star and friend's ability to pull it off. It had been one of the main reasons he had been so keen to work with Sly in the first place. As Jason said, 'No, that's why you choose to work with people that know what they're doing. I mean a lot of the time we don't have the luxury of that choice. But watching Sly,' he added affectionately and respectfully, 'he's the man. It's spitting sawdust with him.'

Ahead of *The Expendables'* official release in the summer of 2010, plenty of journalists were again targeting Sylvester Stallone for glamorising violence on screen. He had faced this sort of criticism before for the *Rambo* films in the 1980s (as had Jason with *The Transporter* and *Crank*) but now there seemed to be an understandable, more sensitive form of anti-violent post-9/11 political correctness. Rather than presenting *The Expendables* in the style of the simplistic good-versus-evil Hollywood action films of the 1980s, Stallone proudly and honestly defended his work.

It was clear that Stallone wasn't trying to address the big political issues of the day. Instead, he wanted to tackle the universal issue of redemption: 'I didn't want to go into something too complex, controversial or politically correct. I wanted it to be old-school,' he told journalists. 'People say it's a throwback but that's all we know. I always try and deal with redemption. I think everyone in this room, and everyone on the planet, has regret ... that at one moment they made the wrong decision that sometimes just never gets your life back on course. This thing with Mickey Rourke, where he goes, "We used to be something, now we're worth nothing because we gave up this ... " It comes back to redemption.'

Alongside this 'redeeming' feature, the film also looked back at the Golden Age of action-adventure movies when, despite the fact that they were in it primarily for the money, even the meanest of mercenaries seemed to have a heart, a sense of honour and a code of conduct. Blurring the boundaries between real-life mercenaries and battle-scarred actors, Stallone wanted to prove that while on-screen violence should be justifiable in terms of good conquering evil, even old action heroes grew old and cynical.

'In fact, in one of the scenes that got cut from the movie we discuss what happened to the code. Jason said to me, "We used to only go after bad people ... " And I replied, "The code died with apathy." It showed my character had stopped caring. But I only ever kill people that need to be killed ... it's killers killing killers. The ones that deserve it get it and they get it good. And the ones that go after women really get it!'

Although some of the early previews treated *The Expendables* as an unwelcome return to the prehistoric age of *Lethal Weapons* and *Die Hards*, without exception they praised Jason's on-screen presence and ability to more than hold his own in such starry, if scary-looking, company.

When Jason was introduced at the lavish movie premiere in London's Leicester Square in August 2010, he received a rapturous reception, resulting in Stallone's gruff but witty response: 'Don't encourage him. He's here to replace me.' Then, after proudly introducing the film, Stallone walked off stage, laughed and shouted at the assembled press, 'None of you are getting your money back!'

Awarding the film four stars out of five in the *Sunday Express*, Brigit Grant declared that 'Sly and the boys explode back ... in a slam-bang action movie shot in sizzling Brazil'. She noted that Stallone, 'refusing to rely on CGI, has everyone doing their own stunts and there are some really impressive ones'. Meanwhile the *Independent* called it 'a retro blast ... one of the year's guiltiest pleasures; a testosterone overload that recalls the era of cinema when men were men and women needed rescuing'.

Most British newspapers generally agreed: '*The Expendables* does exactly what it says on the label, offering a nostalgic and very violent reminder of the late 80s/early 90s action films that used to be populated by most of its stars.' Or, '*The Expendables* entertains in an old-school kind of way by placing its stars centre-stage and playing to their strengths, as opposed to the special effects department.'

Entertainment Weekly declared that 'Sylvester Stallone has made a movie that blows up real good'. The JoBlo.com website claimed it was 'the manliest movie ever made', while Movie-Web described it as 'a sweet infusion of glorious violence and mayhem; a hard-hitting, unrepentant action extravaganza!'

Even some of those who had clearly expected to hate this return to the action-adventure dark ages found themselves appreciating certain elements of the film. Realising that we now 'live in a world in which the movies' biggest action heroes are played by pantywaists like Robert Downey Jnr and Christian Bale, proper actors whose biggest muscles are inside their heads', Genevieve Harrison of *Empire* magazine concluded that '*The Expendables* does what it says on the tin; it delivers a super-size portion of bone-cracking, bullet-spraying, muscle-flexing, head-exploding action, thankfully with the kind of tongue-in-cheek ironic distance which was fatally absent from Stallone's last directorial outing, the ill-advised, ill-fated *Rambo*.'

Success or failure? Of course, the final decision would not be made by the critics or the market researchers, but simply by counting the number of bottoms on cinema seats at the box office. In America it spent two weeks at number one in the box office charts, bringing in a quick $100 million. Within the first three months of *The Expendables*' release, Stallone's $80million film had generated over $225million worldwide and there were already discussions about the production of *The Expendables 2*.

Sylvester Stallone, the battle-scarred prize-fighter, had made another astonishing cinematic comeback. And alongside him, modestly taking most of the plaudits and critically central to the film's great commercial triumph, stood his successor Jason Statham. In his early days as an action hero, Jason had lazily been branded the 'British Bruce Willis', a shaven-headed muscle-bound copy of the *Die Hard* legend. Now, in 2010, two of his movie heroes – Bruce Willis and Sylvester Stallone – gave him their official professional and personal seals of approval.

When, in October 2010, *GQ* magazine named Jason as one of their 'Men of the Year', they pointed out that in *The*

217

Expendables 'Sylvester Stallone is effectively anointing Jason Statham as Hollywood's new action hero'. As *GQ*'s editor Dylan Jones wrote, 'Jason Statham is Britain's most unsung, yet most consistently successful actor working in Hollywood today ... *The Transporter, Crank, Mean Machine, The Bank Job, Death Race, The Expendables* ... you only need to glance at the titles to work out that Statham has made a wedge for himself by being Britain's best bare-knuckle badass – truly cinema's last action hero.'

CONCLUSION:

TO INFINITY AND BEYOND

In the second decade of the 21st century, Jason Statham finds himself ranked among the top ten Hollywood box office leading men, alongside major American stars such as Leonardo DiCaprio, Johnny Depp, Will Smith, Jim Carrey, Robert Downey Jnr, George Clooney, Brad Pitt, Sylvester Stallone and Tom Hanks. In the ten years since he first relocated to Los Angeles, hoping to build on the success of his roles in Guy Ritchie's *Lock Stock & Two Smoking Barrels* and *Snatch*, Jason has become one of the most consistently successful movie stars on the planet.

The figures speak for themselves. Of the twenty-four films he had appeared in between 1998 and 2010, the vast majority had enhanced Jason's reputation as an actor and, increasingly, as a bankable star. With box-office receipts approaching $2billion worldwide to his name, he had conquered Hollywood and convinced the leading producers and studios that he was one of the actors most likely to deliver a profitable major movie.

Those who had doubted Jason's talent, who'd felt he had risen without trace, would now struggle hard to question his A-list status. Moving stealthily from *The Transporter* through to *The Expendables*, Jason suddenly found himself in the unusual youthful company of Daniel Radcliffe and Robert Pattinson as Britain's leading male film exports. And with tough-guy Americans falling by the wayside and Daniel Craig's future as James Bond in doubt, Jason had suddenly become the greatest action-adventure hero of his generation.

Of course, he would modestly take the accolade in his stride. 'It's a pretty big title that, but it's great to hear. You can never get too carried away with it because it is a harsh industry and what goes up must come down. You have to be prepared that if you make too many bad choices then that is the end of the road. So you need to be optimistic and confident that you won't make that many wrong decisions.'

In terms of action films, no other Hollywood star has a comparable track record. With the international economic crisis spreading like Californian wildfire through the incredibly expensive world of Hollywood film production – causing delays to the next Bourne production and resulting in the cancellation of the twenty-third James Bond movie due to MGM's bankruptcy – it seems significant that Jason finds himself increasingly in demand. The credit crunch had definitely not affected his career opportunities.

Although his professional fame and personal fortune has mainly been built in the action genre, Jason refused to rest on his laurels and continued to fight against being typecast in the same way that his friends, heroes, and now admirers,

Sylvester Stallone and Bruce Willis, were pigeon-holed in the 1980s. The key deciding factor seemed to be if it had a good story, Jason would be interested.

'I've got an open mind when it comes to cinema,' he had once said. 'I love comedies, I love great dramas, thrillers ... I love them all. As long as the role is good and they want me in it. If the script is good and it interests you and you think you can do something then why not go ahead? ... Ideally I'd want to do something that's a bit more of an adult movie in tone, like the Bourne movies, but maybe that's not what the people want to see. I dunno, it's hard. You always want to do what you haven't done.'

He had already worked on films in a wide variety of genres – science fiction, gangster comedy, war movies, drama, thrillers, martial arts, action and fantasy – and few of his competitors or contemporaries could compete with this versatility. Looking to continue in the same vein, on the immediate horizon, Jason is centrally involved in five remarkably diverse films for 2011 – *The Mechanic, Blitz, Safe, The Killer Elite* and the animated comedy, *Gnomeo and Juliet*.

First of all, there is his starring role as Arthur Bishop in *The Mechanic*, which is based on the 1972 Charles Bronson movie about an experienced assassin who trains up a young apprentice to take over from him. Made by Millennium with support from CBS Films, it has been described as 'a strong, intelligent action thriller' by CBS President Amy Baer. Shot in Louisiana, Virginia, Michigan and Washington, *The Mechanic* would be released in January 2011, and directed by Simon West, who had made *Con Air, When a Stranger Calls* and the original *Lara Croft: Tomb Raider*.

The film also stars Ben Foster (who appeared in *The*

Messenger) and Jason's veteran *Italian Job* co-star, the charismatic Donald Sutherland. An early *Mechanic* trailer featured Jason explaining that his role was about 'a guy who fixes problems', with dramatic on-screen captions detailing the hit-man's rules of engagement: 'Never get too close ... Never leave a trace ... Know your place ... Always leave your mark.' Another gritty thriller, starring Jason and ready for release in 2011, would be *Blitz*. Based on the book of the same name by the Irish crime writer Ken Bruen, Jason plays Detective Sergeant Brant, a tough London cop trying to track down a serial killer who is targeting police officers. Directed by Elliott Lester, *Blitz* also featured Paddy Considine (*The Bourne Ultimatum*), David Morrissey (*The Reaping, Captain Corelli's Mandolin*) and Aiden Gillen from *The Wire*.

Post-*Expendables*, Jason had also been busy in the autumn of 2010 filming Boaz Yakin's *Safe* in New York's Chinatown. Yakin is the highly regarded young director of *Uptown Girls*, *Prince of Persia: The Sands of Time* and, particularly, *Remember the Titans*. Rumoured to be a *Bourne*-style thriller with plenty of action and violence, *Safe*'s producers include Jason's manager Steve Chasman and also the Hollywood actor/producer Kevin Spacey of *American Beauty*, *L.A. Confidential* and *Usual Suspects* fame. While working on the film in New York, Jason decided to extend his small property empire by scouting for a Manhattan apartment in Greenwich Village with his new girlfriend, Rosie Huntington-Whiteley.

Surely the most eagerly awaited of Jason's 2011 films would be *The Killer Elite*, in which he stars alongside another of his heroes, Robert De Niro. Starting out in London-based gangland films, Jason's had expressed admiration for De

Niro's great performances in the genre's classics such as *Goodfellas* and *Casino*.

After working with Stallone, Schwarzenegger and Willis on *The Expendables*, he was equally thrilled to be working with De Niro on location in Australia. Speaking of his co-stars De Niro and Clive Owen, Jason said, 'Those guys you can really bounce off – improvise – do something with a little depth. And Bobby De Niro – it doesn't get much better than that. Most of the time I'll have hairdressers cast opposite me. Now it's Oscar-winners!'

Having been put through a gruelling training programme for *Death Race* by the former Navy SEAL Logan Hood, in *The Killer Elite* Jason now found himself portraying an ex-Navy SEAL called Danny Bryce, who is forced out of retirement to rescue an ex-colleague in danger (Spike, played by Clive Owen). According to a report in *Variety*, the film is based on real events that were the subject of Sir Ranulph Fiennes' work of fiction, *The Feather Men*, published in 1991. A synopsis of Fiennes' novel explained that the Feather Men were a vigilante group dedicated to solving crimes that the police could not. In particular, Fiennes' book detailed the Feather Men's fourteen-year struggle to capture the Clinic, a band of contract killers who murdered four former British soldiers.

Shot in Victoria, Australia and Glamorgan, Wales, it is a $29million first feature from the Irish-born director Gary McKendry. It is produced by Omnilab Media, one of the companies that had helped to fund Jason's *The Bank Job* back in 2008. Contrary to many Hollywood rumours, this *Killer Elite* is no relation to Sam Peckinpah's 1975 spy thriller of the same name.

Jason's manager Steve Chasman had always believed that Statham could turn his hand to any genre, but he also commented, 'You have to keep the audience happy, too, and give the people what they want. We can't forget we are making movies for people, not just for ourselves. Is Jason going to go off and do Shakespeare? I don't think so, at least not right now.'

If Jason had ever really wanted to perform Shakespeare, then surely the most bizarre and unexpected film he would ever become involved with would be the weird-sounding animation *Gnomeo and Juliet*. Yes, it's a version of *Romeo and Juliet* acted by garden gnomes.

Back in 2008, having been disappointed with his performance in the finished version of the video-game-based *In the Name of the King: A Dungeon Siege Tale*, Jason had nevertheless expressed a real interest in participating in animated films and, in particular, Pixar-style productions. 'I really have tried,' he had said. 'I've auditioned a few times for animation, and I never quite got it. Every time I got pipped to the post, but I would love to. *Love to*. Any of those big animation films I love. It's something that's on the list of things to do.'

In *Gnomeo and Juliet*, Jason voices the ill-fated Shakespearean character Tybalt, alongside James McAvoy's Gnomeo and Emily Blunt's Juliet. The impressive all-star cast of gnome voices also includes Sir Michael Caine, Dame Maggie Smith, Patrick Stewart, Julie Walters, Hulk Hogan, Dolly Parton, Matt Lucas and Ozzy Osbourne. Co-produced by Sir Elton John and his partner David Furnish's company Rocket Pictures together with Miramax, the gnomic CGI-animated feature would not adhere very closely to Shakespeare's original concept.

Directed by *Shrek 2*'s Kelly Asbury, the advance trailer confirmed that 'You'll experience Shakespeare's legendary tale as you've never seen it before.' Apparently, Gnomeo and Juliet get caught up in a neighbourly Montagues-versus-Capulets conflict between red-hatted and blue-hatted garden gnomes. However, the plot also involves pink plastic flamingos and lawn mowers.

Approaching his fortieth birthday (in September 2012), it sometimes seems as if Jason's all-consuming commitment to work, his unblinking focus on his film career, dominates all other aspects of his life. One wonders if he fears resting for too long, as if the world might stop, he'll wake up and the incredible Hollywood dream might be over. Examining his back-breaking schedule and the number of film projects he is rumoured to be involved with, the key question surely must be 'If and when does The Stath sleep?'

As if *Safe*, *Blitz*, *The Killer Elite*, *The Mechanic* and so on were not enough to keep a confirmed insomniac and workaholic busy for the next five years, Jason would also be closely linked with three more films for 2011 and 2012. According to some Hollywood pre-production sources, he is set to appear in a 1930s-based gangster movie *Pretty Baby Machine* alongside his *Expendables* and *13* co-star Mickey Rourke, plus Ian McShane (who had been in *Death Race* with him) and Gary Oldman, a long-time associate of Jason's friend Luc Besson.

Based on a graphic novel and set in the USA during Prohibition in 1933, *Pretty Baby Machine* focuses on a triumvirate of gangsters – Pretty Boy Floyd, Baby Face Nelson and Machine Gun Kelly – who are all trying to outwit Al

Capone and carve out a piece of the Chicago action while John Dillinger languishes in jail.

Then there's *Potsdamer Platz*, to be directed by Tony Scott (*Man on Fire*, *Top Gun*) and produced by his brother Ridley Scott (*American Gangster*, *Gladiator*) – a $38million drama about two members of a New Jersey-based crime family looking to expand internationally. Due to start shooting in Puerto Rico in January 2011, the film's unconfirmed cast is rumoured to feature Jason, Mickey Rourke, Javier Bardem and Christopher Walken.

However, the idea Jason seemed most keen on would be *The Grabbers*, a film project he had been developing with Steve Chasman. They were still trying to secure the financing for it when Jason spoke about it in 2009. 'We've got a movie we're trying to do, written by David and Janet Peoples, in the vein of an old film, *The Treasure of Sierra Madre*. It's not a remake or anything but it's a little bit like that, about relationships and how greed contaminates the relationships these three people have. The working title is *The Grabbers*.'

The involvement of David and Janet Peoples would obviously be a key factor in Jason's interest in this idea. David Peoples had written many classic films including *Blade Runner*, *Unforgiven*, *Hero* (which starred Dustin Hoffman) and, together with Janet, the apocalyptic Bruce Willis vehicle *Twelve Monkeys*.

Given the position Jason now finds himself in – an incredibly wealthy and successful movie star with an envious lifestyle and a beautiful girlfriend in Rosie Huntington-Whiteley – it seems unusual that he still has the drive to work so incredibly hard. But as he once said back in 2005, after making *Revolver*, 'It's not all about success and winning.

It's not all about power and money. Now it's good to have no concerns and no worries, to take care of your family, to use what you gain from success, but also it's still best to be aware that's not going to be the most important thing in your life. You have to keep working, you have to take risks, that's what it's all about and success will come if you have that outlook.'

It would be convenient to analyse his 'keep working' ethic and philosophy in the context of his street-hustling working-class background, and to suggest that by making three or four films a year he might have been over-compensating for his youthful failure – by his own high standards – to win an Olympic gold medal as a diver.

But, escaping from his past and relishing the new environment he now thrived in, Jason clearly felt he was approaching the peak of his powers and was willing to grasp every great new opportunity and enjoy his career. He hadn't forgotten where he had come from or how privileged he now was to be successfully pursuing his Hollywood dream.

'I prefer to be busy,' he had said in 2007. 'I like working. It's great. To me it's a privilege to be coming out and working with new faces. It's a lot of fun. I mean the big kid inside comes out, and you get to be somebody else for a few months.' ... It's not like we work seven days a week. There's a lot of people digging roads out there. I'm sure they'd be happy doing what I'm doing, so I try to not ever get jaded and start moaning about, "Oh, I'm a little bit tired, I want to go home." We've been privileged really to be able to come out and make movies. So I'm never one to moan. But I like being busy. I hate sitting around. It becomes too destructive.'

It's unlikely that Jason will be sitting around much during the coming years. In addition to the films already in production, let's not forget that he also has his established franchises to take care of. It's more than likely that he will return as Frank Martin in *Transporter 4* in the not-too-distant future, and there is also a strong possibility that he will play the hyperactive Chev Chelios once again in *Crank 3*. 'I know Neveldine and Taylor [the directors] are definitely talking about a third film,' he said recently, 'but I have no idea what their story would be yet.'

Even more certain, given its extraordinary success at the worldwide box office, Jason will surely be guaranteed top billing when Sylvester Stallone regroups his battle-scarred troops for *Expendables 2*. How could he refuse Sly's offer? He would describe Stallone as 'an inspiration to everyone in action movies ... when you're with him it's like you're with Elvis Presley!'

Bruce Willis, who has already been signed up to play a villain in the sequel, revealed that Stallone is 'going for all the marbles this time and is going to get everybody in'. By this, Willis means every fit and able movie action hero available – perhaps even including Jean-Claude Van Damme, Steven Seagal and Kurt Russell, who had all chosen not to appear in the first film.

As Charisma Carpenter, who played Jason's girlfriend in *The Expendables*, said, 'Right now I'm hoping *The Expendables* is super-successful so we do an *Expendables 2* and then there goes my film career off and running!' Charisma wasn't alone in her enthusiasm for the franchise. 'I hope so,' commented Brigit Grant of the *Sunday Express*, 'and hopefully a set of Expendable dolls for senior citizens to collect.'

Whereas most successful film stars seem content if one or two meaty roles come along in the course of their career, it's interesting that Jason is always on the look out for further franchises to explore. He has clearly learnt from his hero and colleague Sly Stallone that there is plenty of box-office mileage in developing strong characters such as John Rambo and Rocky Balboa over a long-running series of movies.

'There's a couple of things out there,' he had cautiously commented in 2008, refusing to mention names in case he was tempting fate and the projects never happened. 'There's a few cool things that I know that I'd be really good for. There's a possible chance they might come my way and, if they do, then both of them have great potential to be great franchises. It's always good to do franchises, all the big action stuff. Sly's done a few, they work well. The *Die Hards*, the *Lethal Weapons*. You get a good one and you can keep 'em going.'

One franchise he had definitely been exploring was *The Equalizer*, based on the Michael Sloan-created TV series from the late 1980s starring Edward Woodward. In many ways, Woodward's character Robert McCall was as complex and fascinating as Jason's Frank Martin in *The Transporter*. Both had unspoken, troubled and mysterious pasts and both were available for hire as trouble-shooters, protectors or investigators. They operated outside the law but acted with cool, stylish, moral judgement against gangsters, rapists and other ruthless criminals.

Jason confirmed, in 2008, that *The Equalizer* was one of the franchises he had been discussing with the film mogul Harvey Weinstein: 'I saw Harvey the other week and he was talking to me about that. It's a great one.' However, Jason would face tough competition from Russell Crowe, who is also firmly in the frame to play Robert McCall.

Perhaps Jason's biggest box-office success, up there in terms of profits with *The Expendables*, was his role as Handsome Rob in the 2003 remake of *The Italian Job*, which had first introduced him as a character actor to a huge new audience in the USA. Having generated over $180million worldwide, inevitably the production company Paramount was desperate for a sequel. Not to be confused with Jason's 2008 British *Sweeney*-style drama *The Bank Job*, for years there have been constant rumours that a film titled *The Brazilian Job*, reuniting the original cast, will soon go into production.

Although he had been incredibly positive about the prospect, Jason explained that it would never be as simple or straightforward as the producers hoped. 'That's a little more complicated,' he said, 'because there are more people's schedules to run together. So I don't know how that's going to play out. But I'm good friends with Charlize [Theron] and Mark [Wahlberg] and Seth [Green] and Mos [Def] – and they all want to do it.' So with all the cast members keen at the prospect, we can hope that it is a matter of when rather than if. As Jason said 'it's the best fun in the world, and for me to turn my nose up at the opportunity of doing a great movie with great actors ... Yeah, I'll do as many as they want me to do.'

Of course, the most consistently successful source for film franchises throughout the 2000s has been the superhero stories based on Marvel and DC comic characters; clearly, they have replaced the big-budget action-adventure movies that were so popular with cinema audiences in the 1980s and 1990s. The *Batman*, *Spider-Man*, *Iron Man*, *X-Men* and *Fantastic Four* franchises have dominated cinema box offices in recent years. For example, the 2008 version of *Iron Man* starring Robert Downey Jnr cost about $140million to make but generated more than $570million in receipts. In the light of these highly profitable figures, it's little wonder that Jason has often been linked with any number of superhero projects in development. The obvious rumour, because of his swimming and diving past, was that he would be signed up to play the scantily clad Prince Namor, *The Submariner* from the Marvel stories. But, amusingly, he denied this: 'I don't know if I'd look right running around in a tight Speedo with wings on my ankles.' Instead, later reports suggest that David Boreanaz, who had played Angel in *Buffy the Vampire Slayer*, would be the favourite for the underwater role.

Jason has, however, expressed an interest in reviving the role of Daredevil, even though Ben Affleck had appeared as the film superhero as recently as 2003. 'I'm a big comic-book fan and *Daredevil* – that movie that got made a few years ago – I thought they could have done a better job with that. If somebody wants to put Frank Miller and me together and do one, let's have a look at the script.'

Miller was the film-maker and comics specialist who had worked for Marvel from 1979 onwards. As the writer of the 'born again' storyline, he had rejuvenated the lesser superhero character Daredevil, a.k.a. Matt Murdock, who had been originally created in 1964.

When the *LA Times* did get Jason together with Frank Miller, in a bar of the Hard Rock Hotel in San Diego, July 2008, Jason was asked if a British actor really could wear the red horns of the 'Man without Fear'? 'Absolutely, just give me the chance. I would love to be Daredevil!'

Quite when Jason would fit this stint as a superhero into his hectic schedule remains unclear, particularly as he had also expressed interest in another graphic-novel-based character, *The Crow*. Originally made famous by Bruce Lee's son Brandon in the 1994 movie adaptation, *The Crow* was a dark fantasy about Eric Draven, a rock musician who returned from the dead to avenge his own murder and the brutal rape and death of his girlfriend.

'I'm trying to think of what would be a good comic-book character for me to play,' Jason once said, without tempting fate. 'You know, there's talk of them redoing *The Crow*. That was a good movie with Brandon Lee, although that was years ago. So if that one comes my way ... bang!'

The 2012 remake of *The Crow* was originally going to be directed by Stephen Norrington with a screenplay by the rock star Nick Cave. But Norrington apparently left after an unnamed actor got involved and asked for a re-write. At one stage, Mark Wahlberg or Ethan Peck were also both rumoured to be favourites to take the Brandon Lee role, but nothing has been confirmed.

As Jason knew well, rumoured projects might not necessarily come to fruition. For example, back in 2003 – at around the time he had completed *The Italian Job* – there had been talk of him co-starring with George Clooney on *The Fall Guy*. Based on the 1980s TV series starring Lee Majors, it would have featured Clooney as the stuntman and bounty hunter Colt Seavers, with Jason as Colt's sidekick Howie. Eight years on, Dreamworks still have the idea on option but there is no sign that the project is about to receive the crucial green light.

It would surely seem much more likely – given their impressive creative track record together in the early years of their careers – that Jason would soon work again with his old friend Guy Ritchie. Having starred in several Ritchie productions, Jason often expressed his gratitude to – and admiration for – Guy. It was a firm friendship that had helped Jason both professionally and personally, particularly following his break-up with Kelly Brook. For all the flaws and disappointments with *Revolver* in 2005, both Jason and Guy had still regarded the experience as a brave and rewarding exercise, even though for several years afterwards it certainly affected Guy's reputation as a writer-director.

While Jason had steadily built his own star status through *The Transporter*, *Crank*, *The Italian Job*, *The Bank Job*, *Cellular*, *Chaos* and *The Expendables*, Guy Ritchie had struggled to rediscover his early form. After the commercial failure of *Revolver*, his next film, *RocknRolla* (2008) – starring Gerard Butler, Tom Wilkinson, Mark Strong and Thandie Newton – barely broke even. *RocknRolla* also featured Tom Hardy as a character called Handsome Bob, probably based on Jason's *Italian Job* character Handsome Rob. Some critics even wondered if Jason had turned down the role.

Ritchie, however, would have a huge success in 2009 with his Oscar-nominated big-budget production of *Sherlock Holmes* starring Robert Downey Jnr and Jude Law. Made at a cost of $90million, the film returned $518million at the box office. Back in demand and once again a leading player in the British and American film industry, Guy now has several major projects in development and pre-production. One of these, *Gamekeeper*, is based on his own series of graphic novels about an estate worker in Scotland called Brock, who seeks revenge for the mysterious death of his laird and friend Jonah Morgan at the hands of Russian paramilitary mercenaries. Having played the stylish tweed-coated country gent for the hare-coursing scene in *Snatch*, off duty from promoting boxing, some have speculated as to whether Jason would be the ideal candidate for Brock.

Although the *Sun* would report that Guy Ritchie and Jason were reuniting to work on a new musical that was, one unbelievable insider source suggested, 'a cross between Worzel Gummidge and *Bullitt!*', this may well refer to Guy's undeveloped film idea *Lobo*, based on the DC Comics drama about an alien bounty hunter. It would seem more likely that they would either get together on *Sherlock Holmes 2* or, perhaps, Guy's proposed Hollywood version of the King Arthur and the Knights of the Round Table legend.

Backed by Warner Brothers, and with a script by Warren Ellis (who wrote *RED* for Bruce Willis), Guy Ritchie's *Excalibur* (scheduled for 2012) will be based on the Arthurian romances written by Sir Thomas Malory in 1485, focusing on the life of the legendary 6th-century Celtic king who defeated Saxon invaders. The *Independent* has already described the proposed film as 'The Magnificent Seven in armour'. It sounds right up Jason's street.

Aside from Guy Ritchie, there are also plenty of productions in development under the auspices of some of Jason's close friends and champions. Perhaps, returning the favour for turning him into the Transporter, Jason will appear in one of Luc Besson's forthcoming films such as *A Monster in Paris* or *The Mechanics of the Heart*. Plus, there have also been rumours that Jason will make another martial arts movie with his old friend and *Expendables* co-star Jet Li. Following *The One* (2001) and *War* (2007), Jason has spoken of the possibility of a third film to complete the futuristic trilogy. Whatever happens next, whatever the genre, you can guarantee that Jason presence on screen should secure success at the box office. And, who knows, perhaps the opportunity of a lifetime is waiting in the wings.

With the untitled twenty-third James Bond film scheduled for release in 2013 but 'postponed indefinitely' as of April 2010, there is now a serious question mark over Daniel Craig's future as the main man. His initial five-year contract with EON Productions, for the franchise's bankrupt producers MGM, ended in October 2010. The twenty-third Bond film would have been directed by Sam Mendes, but it now seems that both Craig and Mendes have had to move on to other projects.

If it is the end for Craig, then could Jason become the seventh 007? Could he be the first dramatically untrained, distinctly non-posh, truly working-class James Bond? Why not? The man himself has favourably compared the inscrutable Frank Martin of *Transporter* infamy with the shaken-not-stirred secret agent: 'You could say he's almost like a working-class James Bond,' laughed Jason. 'He's like a Bond that drinks Heineken, not Dom Pérignon champagne. He's a little less refined but still very capable.'

So capable, in fact, that when William Hill started taking bets on Daniel Craig's successor, Jason was one of the hot favourites alongside Hugh Jackman, Robert Pattinson, Christian Bale, Will Smith, Clive Owen and Sam Worthington. (The outside bets, at 100–1, include Simon Cowell.)

Of course, it may well be that none of these projects come about. It may all stop tomorrow. But the boy from nowhere is unlikely to go back where he came from. If all else fails then, according to his old South London friend Vinnie Jones, he and Jason are going to set up a pub business together. 'Me and Jay have been talking about it for about a year,'

Vinnie announced. 'We were thinking the *Snatch* bar or something like that, down in Santa Monica. We're going to do it, it's just a question of us finding the time. Jay has been working so much and so have I.'

Perhaps, like off-duty Frank Martin in *The Transporter*, the time will come when Jason takes up fishing or sits in the *Snatch* bar, sipping beer and watching the sun go down on the Pacific. Maybe then he will have time to contemplate his incredible journey from streetwise kid to international diver, from street hustler to male model, from comedy gangster to stunt-driving film star, from movie martial artist to globally renowned daredevil action hero. Along the way he has dated some of the most beautiful women on the planet, driven some of the world's most expensive cars, lived a life that most mortals can only dream of, and worked with some of the greatest names in Hollywood history.

The life so far of Jason Statham has been an extraordinary cinematic story. Maybe, one day, someone might make a film about it.

JASON STATHAM

FILMOGRAPHY

Title: **Lock Stock & Two Smoking Barrels**
Year: 1998
Director: Guy Ritchie
Writer: Guy Ritchie
Certificate: 18
Tagline: They lost half a million at cards but they've still got
   a few tricks up their sleeve
Box Office: $26 million
Character: Bacon

Title: **Snatch**
Year: 2000
Director: Guy Ritchie
Writer: Guy Ritchie
Certificate: 18
Tagline: Stealing stones is hazardous
Box Office: $35 million
Character: Turkish

Title: **Turn It Up**
Year: 2000
Director: Robert Adetuyi
Writers: Ray Daniels, Chris Hudson, Kelly Hilaire and Robert
    Adetuyi
Certificate: 18
Tagline: How you gonna win?
Box Office: $1.5 million
Character: Mr B

Title: **Ghost of Mars**
Year: 2001
Director: John Carpenter
Writers: Larry Sulkis, John Carpenter
Certificate: 15
Tagline: Forget The Rules. Abandon Your Fears. Save Your
    Soul.
Box Office: $8.5 million
Character: Sgt. Jericho Butler

Title: **The One**
Year: 2001
Director: James Wong
Writers: Glen Morgan, James Wong
Certificate: 15
Tagline: In order to save the universe, he will have to fight
    the fiercest enemy he has ever faced ... himself
Box Office: $44 million
Character: MVA Agent Evan Funsh

Title: **Mean Machine**
Year: 2001

Director: Barry Skolnick
Writers: Tracy Keenan Wynn, Charlie Fletcher, Chris Baker and Andrew Day
Certificate: 15
Tagline: It's Not Just About Football, It's About Pride Inside!
Box Office: $1 million
Character: Monk

Title: **The Transporter**
Year: 2001
Directors: Louis Leterrier, Corey Yuen
Writers: Luc Besson, Robert Mark Kamen
Certificate: 15
Tagline: Rules are made to be broken
Box Office: $25.5 million
Character: Frank Martin

Title: **The Italian Job**
Year: 2003
Director: F. Gary Gray
Writers: Troy Kennedy-Martin, Donna Powers and Wayne Powers
Certificate: 12A
Tagline: Get in. Get out. Get even.
Box Office: $168 million
Character: Handsome Rob

Title: **Collateral**
Year: 2004
Director: Michael Mann
Writer: Stuart Beattie
Certificate: 15

Tagline: It started like any other night
Box Office:
Character: Airport Man

Title: **Cellular**
Year: 2004
Director: David R Ellis
Writers: Larry Cohen and Chris Morgan
Certificate: 15
Tagline: If the signal dies so does she
Box Office: $35 million
Character: Ethan

Title: **Transporter 2**
Year: 2005
Director: Louis Leterrier
Writers: Luc Besson, Robert Mark Kamen
Certificate: 15
Tagline: The best in the business is back in the game
Box Office: $45 million
Character: Frank Martin

Title: **London**
Year: 2005
Director: Hunter Richards
Writer: Hunter Richards
Certificate: 18
Tagline: A film about love and her victims
Box Office: $0.5 million
Character: Bateman

Title: **Revolver**
Year: 2005
Director: Guy Ritchie
Writers: Luc Besson and Guy Ritchie
Certificate: 15
Tagline: Your mind will not accept a game this big
Box Office: $2 million
Character: Jake Green

Title: **Chaos**
Year: 2005
Director: Tony Giglio
Writer: Tony Giglio
Certificate: 15
Tagline: When the system breaks down ... someone is about
    to get rich
Box Office: $12 million
Character: Quentin Conners

Title: **Crank**
Year: 2006
Directors: Mark Neveldine, Brian Taylor
Writers: Mark Neveldine, Brian Taylor
Certificate: 18
Tagline: ?
Box Office:
Character: Chev Chelios

Title: **In the Name of the King: A Dungeon Siege Tale**
Year: 2007
Director: Uwe Boll

Writers: Doug Taylor, Jason Rappaport, Don Stroncak and
  Chris Taylor
Certificate: 12
Tagline: Rise and Fight
Box Office: $4 million
Character: Farmer

Title: **War**
Year: 2007
Director: Philip G. Atwell
Writers: Lee Anthony Smith, Gregory J. Bradley
Certificate: 18
Tagline: Vengeance is the ultimate weapon
Box Office: $22.5 million
Character: Crawford

Title: **The Bank Job**
Year: 2008
Director: Roger Donaldon
Writers: Dick Clement, Ian la Frenais
Certificate: 15
Tagline: The true story of a heist gone wrong ... in all the
  right ways
Box Office: $31 million
Character: Terry Leather

Title: **Death Race**
Year: 2008
Director: Paul W. S. Anderson
Writers: Paul W. S. Anderson, Robert Thorn, Charles B.
  Griffith and Ib Melchior

Certificate: 15
Tagline: This Friday, may the best man live
Box Office: $75 million
Character: Jensen Ames

Title: **Transporter 3**
Year: 2008
Director: Olivier Megaton
Writers: Luc Besson, Robert Mark Kamen
Certificate: 15
Tagline: This time, the rules are the same. Except One.
Box Office: $34 million
Character: Frank Martin

Title: **Crank: High Voltage**
Year: 2009
Directors: Mark Neveldine, Brian Taylor
Writer: Mark Neveldine, Brian Taylor
Certificate: 18
Tagline: Stay Charged, Stay Alive!
Box Office: $30 million
Character: Chev Chelios

Title: **13**
Year: 2010
Director: Géla Babluani
Writers: Géla Babluani, Greg Pruss
Certificate: Not released
Tagline: Not released
Box Office: not available
Character: Jasper

Title: **The Expendables**
Year: 2010
Director: Sylvester Stallone
Writers: Dave Callahan, Sylvester Stallone
Certificate: 15
Tagline: Choose Your Weapon
Box Office: $224 million
Character: Lee Christmas

Title: **Blitz**
Year: 2010
Director: Elliot Lester
Writers: Ken Bruen, Nathan Parker
Certificate: Not released
Tagline: Not released
Box Office:
Character: Not released

Films in Production:
Title: **Gnomeo & Juliet**
Director: Kelly Asbury
Character: Tybalt

Title: **The Mechanic**
Director: Simon West
Character: Arthur Bishop

Title: **The Killer Elite**
Director: Gary McKendry
Character: Danny Bryce

Title: **Safe**
Director: Boaz Yakin